THE EFFECTS OF FOOD PRICE AND SUBSIDY POLICIES ON EGYPTIAN AGRICULTURE

Joachim von Braun
Hartwig de Haen

Research Report 42
International Food Policy Research Institute
November 1983

Library of Congress Cataloging
in Publication Data

Von Braun, Joachim, 1950-
    The effects of food price and subsidy policies
on Egyptian agriculture.

    (Research report ; 42)
    Bibliography: p. 89.
    1. Food prices—Government policy—Egypt.
2. Agricultural price supports—Egypt. 3. Agriculture and state—Egypt. I. Haen, Hartwig de. II. Title.
III. Series: Research report (International Food
Policy Research Institute) ; 42.

HD9017.E4V66 1983   338.1'0962   83-22829
ISBN 0-89629-043-3

CONTENTS

TABLES

FOREWORD

Food prices are a major factor in determining incentives to agricultural producers and the level of real income and nutritional status of low-income consumers. Explicit food subsidies allow lower food prices to consumers relative to producer prices than would otherwise be the case. Nevertheless, there has been concern that food subsidies may in effect be paid for by farmers and hence serve as a disincentive to agricultural production. This report by Joachim von Braun and Hartwig de Haen analyzes this issue through analysis of a wealth of data and the use of innovative methodological approaches. It examines in particular the effects of agricultural price policies on both consumers and producers, on fiscal resources, and on the income burden placed on agriculture.

The analysis is part of a series of research reports by IFPRI addressing the effects of food subsidy policies on food consumption, nutrition, income distribution, and macroeconomic developments. These studies cover a wide range of countries in Asia, Latin America and Africa and are expected to culminate in a major policy-oriented synthesis. Egypt, because of the large size of its food subsidy programs, is the subject of an intensive, interacting set of studies of food subsidies. These studies, in collaboration with the Institute of National Planning in Cairo and financed by a research contract from the U.S. Agency for International Development, are coordinated by Per Pinstrup-Andersen, director of IFPRI's Food Consumption and Nutrition Policy Program.

Two other reports have been published from this project: *Egypt's Food Subsidy and Rationing System: A Description,* Research Report 34, which is an analytical description of the subsidy system in Egypt, by Harold Alderman, Joachim von Braun, and Sakr Ahmed Sakr, and *Food Subsidies in Egypt: Their Impact on Foreign Exchange and Trade,* Research Report 40, in which Grant Scobie assesses the macroeconomic implications of the food subsidy policy. Results from analyses of the distribution of benefits and costs of the subsidy system will be published in a subsequent report.

John W. Mellor

Washington, D.C.
November 1983

ACKNOWLEDGMENTS

The authors gratefully acknowledge the advice of Ismail Badawy, Ahmed A. Gaffar, Kamal El Ganzouri, and Yahya Mohie El-Din. Fundamental guidance was also provided by Ahmed Goueli. Many of the analytical tools used for this study were developed for a joint project of the Institute of Agricultural Economics, at the University of Gottingen, and the Institute of National Planning, Cairo, which was funded by the Volkswagen Foundation. This research was continued through a project funded by the U.S. Agency for International Development, under the technical supervision of the AID/USDA Nutrition Economics Group.

The authors are also grateful for the help of the researchers in the Agricultural Planning Center of the Institute of National Planning. Most of the data used were provided by the Ministry of Agriculture, the Ministry of Supply and Home Trade, and the Central Agency for Public Mobilization and Statistics in Cairo.

1

SUMMARY

Subsidies to consumers have long been a part of Egypt's social policy, but early in the 1970s government expenditures on food subsidies were greatly expanded in response to increased income, population growth, and the dramatic increase in world prices. Throughout the second half of the 1970s and early 1980s, the food subsidy bill accounted for 10 to 15 percent of the government's total expenditure. The aim of this study is to determine how this rapid growth in consumer subsidies has affected agriculture. Therefore, government spending on agriculture is examined, and the government's price policies on inputs and output and its interventions in allocation and marketing are evaluated.

Much research has been done on the implications of Egypt's subsidy scheme for economic growth and income distribution. In view of the weaknesses inherent in macroeconomic models, such as general equilibrium models, this study relies instead on microeconomic quantitative models.

Inarguably the subsidy system has led to vast increases in food imports, especially grain. This conflicts with Egypt's desire to achieve self-sufficiency. According to a widely held theory, subsidized distribution of imported food tends to depress producer prices, which in turn acts as a disincentive to production and causes crops to be reallocated and farm incomes to be reduced. Income is transferred indirectly from producers to consumers. On the other hand, it may be argued that subsidies represent an increase in real income for consumers that may be spent on additional foods on the open market, which would benefit farmers.

The time-series analysis of major components of the government's budget in this report shows that budgeted food subsidies were negatively correlated with public investment (−0.74), but public nonagricultural investment continued to grow during the mid-1970s when subsidies were rising sharply. The correlation coefficient was 0.71. A regression model of the government's agricultural spending behavior during the entire period 1965-80 shows that a 10 percent increase in the share of food subsidies in the total budget would cause agriculture's share of the budget to decline by 1.4 percent.

Since 1973, however, total spending on agriculture has grown faster than the total budget, mainly because input subsidies have grown at about the same rate as food subsidies. Thus, subsidies to producers have to some extent balanced negative income effects resulting from depressed food prices.

The study also analyzes how agricultural price policy evolved while food subsidies were expanding. The instruments used by the government to intervene in agriculture include controls on imports and exports, compulsory delivery quotas, area allotment, input subsidies, and dual pricing on commodity markets.

A comprehensive model is applied to quantify the effects on agricultural production of current policies, including a policy that would permit all input and output prices to draw closer to international prices. Partial analyses demonstrate that both wheat and rice production respond readily to changes in prices. It appears that there would be significant gains for producers if the gap between international prices, on the one hand, and subsidized consumer prices, government procurement prices, and prices on the uncontrolled market, on the other hand, became less distinct.

The protection of livestock and animal products is a major source of price distortions. If the whole set of domestic input and output prices were adjusted to correspond to international prices, Egyptian wheat production might actually decline because its current competitiveness stems from the high value of straw fodder. If meat and dairy products were no longer protected, livestock production would decline, reducing the need for fodder and feed and weakening the incentive to grow wheat. Production of rice, pulses, and cotton would increase under such circumstances.

The effects of price and market intervention policies on agricultural income, on the welfare of producers and consumers, and on the government budget are analyzed to assess the burden subsidies place on agriculture. A partial equilibrium model of the market for each commodity is constructed, which incorporates all of the major instruments of food policy. It indicates that the implicit taxation of producers has been considerably reduced since 1974. Procurement quotas have been reduced or eliminated, and farmers' incomes have risen—mainly as a result of price increases on the domestic open market. Part of the burden of paying for subsidies has shifted from agriculture to the general budget. Between 1977 and 1980 the indirect (implicit) tax on agriculture decreased to about 17 percent, which is similar to the share of public revenues in the GDP. A regression model shows that the objective of shielding domestic prices from international fluctuations and the availability of additional government revenues led to the reduction of the burden on agriculture.

In sum, this study indicates that the expansion of Egypt's food subsidy system in the 1970s was not primarily at the cost of agriculture. Price distortions are an inherent feature of Egypt's agricultural policy, existing long before explicit food subsidies became an important component in government fiscal outlays. Reducing these distortions could help to overcome inefficiencies in Egyptian agriculture.

2

EVALUATING THE EFFECTS OF FOOD SUBSIDIES ON AGRICULTURE

Food subsidies are one of the most prominent features of the Egyptian economy. These subsidies affect various sectors of the economy, but their influence on agriculture, which comprises both consumers and producers and employs a considerable share of the nation's resources, seems particularly strong.[1]

Because of its importance to the economy, the subsidy system has been the subject of much research. The concepts behind Egypt's food policies and prevalent theories about subsidies are reviewed in this chapter, and the strengths and weaknesses of existing macroeconomic models are assessed.

Policy Evaluation

One widely held hypothesis holds that supplies imported for subsidized distribution in domestic markets tend to depress producer prices of competing commodities and that this price depression creates disincentives to production, reallocation of crops, and reduced farm incomes. Lower producer prices cause implicit income transfers from producers to consumers. On the other hand, it can also be argued that food subsidies cause real income transfers to consumers, resulting in increased demand for commodities on the open market, from which the farm sector could gain. Open markets exist for the subsidized commodities themselves where quantities are rationed, such as rice, or where the number of outlets for the commodity is low, such as for wheat in rural areas.

Actually, the microeconomic mechanisms are even more complex when practical policies are taken into account. In order to avoid a decline of production as a conse-quence of price disincentives, the government operates a strictly controlled area allotment scheme for some crops. Moreover, it has established compulsory delivery quotas at prices fixed below the market prices (see Chapter 3). These delivery quotas and area allotments not only help to reduce variability in resource allocation induced by low prices, but they remove, at least potentially, the need to ensure a market surplus by keeping procurement prices close to or above production costs. Hypothetically, there would seem to be a tendency to increase the producer burden (producer rent forgone) when public funds are scarce.

This explains the commodity composition of the procurement program. Those commodities that are strictly rationed at fixed prices on the food distribution side are also strictly controlled on the production side. Rice, pulses, and sugar are examples. Nonrationed or not strictly rationed commodities like wheat, maize, sorghum, and meat have experienced considerably less interference in allocation and marketing.[2] Agricultural input and output prices are distorted in another way: whereas field crops are usually taxed, the production of meat and milk has typically been protected by import restrictions and by the supply of subsidized feed. The special situation for feed and livestock indicates that food policy may cause a consumer-to-producer transfer and even a producer-to-producer transfer, which accompanies redistribution of incomes among the production sectors within agriculture.

Another line of reasoning focuses on the direct fiscal implications of food subsidies and their indirect effects on public spending on agriculture. Increased government outlays for food subsidies may induce relative

---

[1] For a description of the system see Harold Alderman, Joachim von Braun, and Sakr Ahmed Sakr, *Egypt's Food Subsidy and Rationing System: A Description,* Research Report 34 (Washington, D.C.: International Food Policy Research Institute, 1982).

[2] Ibid., p. 53.

or absolute reductions in the agricultural budget and thus have a negative effect on sectoral development. To the extent that public investments in agriculture and rural infrastructure are connected to food subsidies in such a hypothetical relationship, the effect on sectoral growth and employment could be detrimental, particularly in the long run.

An assessment of the effect of food subsidies on agriculture must take account of specific linkages and policy mechanisms. The effects on production of procurement, price fixing, area allotment, and the competition for scarce public funds have to be considered. A distinction has to be made between those markets where subsidized and rationed commodities are released from government outlets and so-called "open" or "free" markets where transactions of food commodities are uncontrolled.

In addition, supplementary empirical analyses are required that describe specifically: how and to what extent a wedge is placed between consumer and producer prices by specific producer price and procurement policies for the various food commodities; to what extent these policies create gains and burdens for producers and consumers; what effects the policy-induced changes in prices and price ratios have on the composition and the level of agricultural production; and whether variations in food subsidies cause adjustments in public agricultural investment and current expenditure.

The objective of this research is to analyze agricultural policymaking in the environment of an extended food subsidy system. Inefficiencies and misallocation of resources in agriculture arising from food subsidies are hidden costs of such systems. However, it is crucial to separate out from the whole bundle of policy goals and related instruments those that are directly or indirectly linked to food subsidies. The basis for this can be provided only by a complete quantitative assessment of a country's agricultural policy and its determinants. The complex institutional and technical structure of Egypt's agricultural sector make this an ambitious task. Some simplifications are unavoidable. Figure 1 roughly outlines the structure of this report and the approach taken to policy evaluation.

Review of Evidence from Macro Models

Conclusions about the macroeconomic effects of subsidies conflict in various models that have been used to evaluate them. Some of the contradictions are due to differences in model assumptions and structures. Others result from differences in the degree of realism achieved in mapping existing subsidies.[3]

The following macroeconomic effects of subsidies are, however, widely accepted. Subsidies lead to a reduction of consumer prices for the subsidized commodities or for commodities produced using subsidized inputs. This price decline affects price ratios and real disposable income. The effect on the price ratio causes a change in the composition of consumption in favor of subsidized goods. The effect on real disposable income causes an increase of real consumer purchasing power and a subsequent increase in total consumption.

One line of argumentation arising from these assumptions states that, given the inelasticity of food demand, the reduction in prices for food leads to an expansion of the demand for other commodities. At a given nominal wage level, this increase in demand causes a multiplier expansion of employment and output in the rest of the economy. This positive growth effect is, however, accompanied by increased imports and hence an expanded foreign deficit.[4]

---

[3] The macroeconomic effects of food subsidies in Egypt have been analyzed by several authors. More recent publications mentioning implications for agriculture of the subsidy system include J. J. Dethier and H. Esfahani, "Macroeffects of Alternative Price Policies in Egypt," Economics Working Paper 188, Agricultural Development Systems Project, Ministry of Agriculture, Cairo, and the University of California-Berkeley, Cairo, September 1981; Richard S. Eckaus and A. Mohie el-Din, "Consequences of Changes in Food Subsidy Policies in Egypt," Working Paper 265, Department of Economics, Massachusetts Institute of Technology, Cambridge, Mass., April 1980; Khalid Ikram, *Egypt: Economic Management in a Period of Transition* (Baltimore, Md.: Johns Hopkins University Press, 1980); Lance Taylor, "Food Subsidies in Egypt," Department of Economics, Massachusetts Institute of Technology, Cambridge, Mass., October 1979 (mimeographed); and World Bank, *Arab Republic of Egypt: Domestic Resource Mobilization and Growth Prospects for the 1980s,* Report 3123EGT (Washington, D.C.: World Bank, 1980).

[4] An analysis of food subsidy impacts on foreign exchange and trade is given in Grant M. Scobie, *Food Subsidies in Egypt: Their Impact on Foreign Exchange and Trade,* Research Report 40 (Washington, D.C.: International Food Policy Research Institute, 1983).

Figure 1—Analytical framework for the analysis of the effects of food subsidies on agriculture

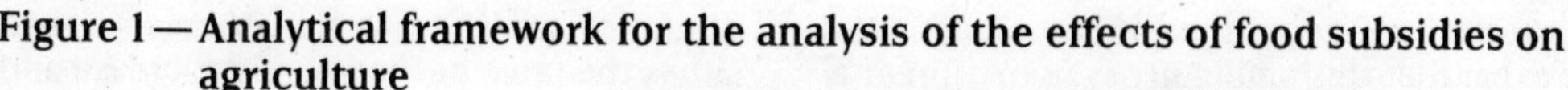

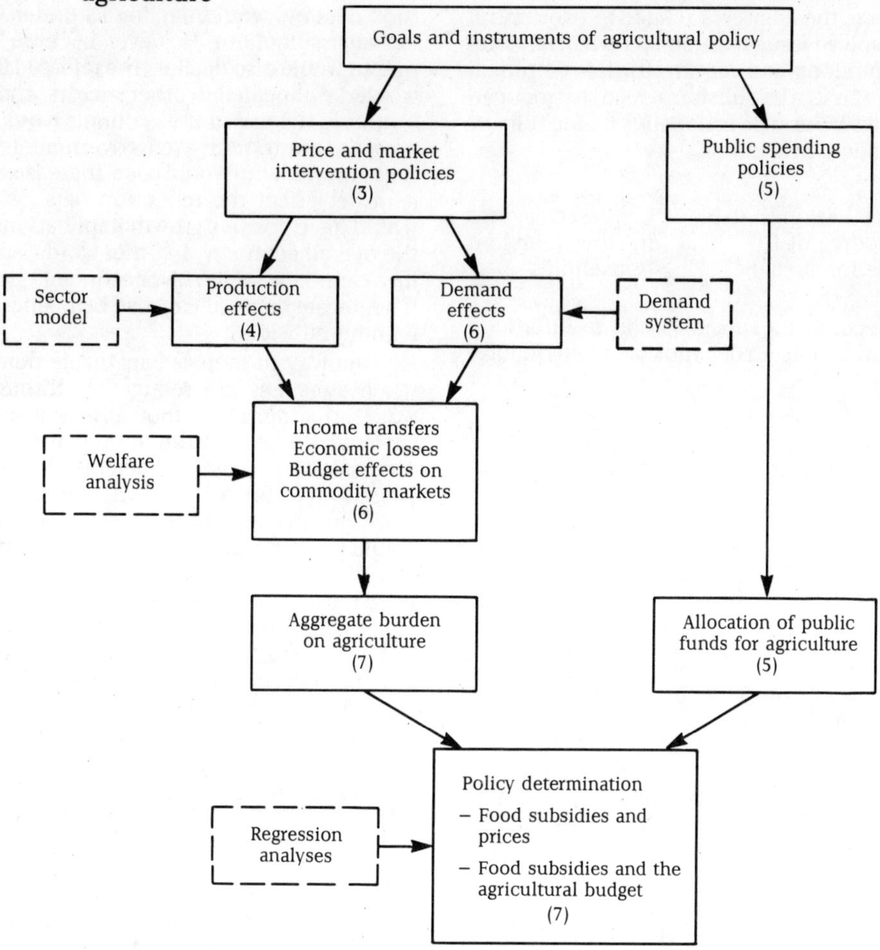

Notes: The numbers in parentheses refer to the chapters of the study. The tools used in this report to analyze the effects on agriculture are outlined with broken lines.

The conclusion to be drawn from this argument built on Keynesian tradition is obvious: a reduction of subsidies would result in an overall contraction of the economy. This kind of economic reasoning is characteristic of the earlier applications of general equilibrium models (GEM): subsidies affect economic activities mainly through their impact on real disposable incomes in conjunction with the price responsiveness of consumer demand.[5] Production levels, imports (which are assumed to be either noncompetitive consumer goods or intermediate inputs in fixed proportion to output), and savings adjust to changes in demand at predetermined investment levels. Total labor supply is assumed to be infinitely elastic at the given wage, which implies free in- and out-migration.

The main controversy about the macroeconomic effects of subsidies relates to the question of whether the subsidies indeed have positive growth effects or whether, as intuitive economic reasoning suggests, they have contractive effects. None of the available models gives a definite answer to this

[5] Eckaus and Mohie el-Din, "Consequences of Changes in Food Subsidy Policies," p. 15.

question. Recent applications of the GEM reveal that this ambiguity is not surprising, because the answer is related to two central unresolved issues, which involve behavioral assumptions and require further empirical tests. First, do subsidies lead to reduced savings? The answer depends on the following inequality:

$$\text{reduced savings at the source of finance for subsidies} \lesseqgtr \text{increased savings in the recipient households}$$

Second, do subsidies add to inflation? The answer again depends on an inequality:

$$\text{inflationary effects of government deficits} \lesseqgtr \text{deflationary effects of price reductions}$$

Both questions are interrelated.[6] If government deficits would indeed be reduced in the absence of subsidies or if subsidies were reduced, the pressure on interest rates and prices might be smaller. This implies that the subsidies that are cut would not be substituted for by other components of aggregate demand and the stated contractive effect would occur. On the other hand, the government would have the chance to substitute for subsidies through increased public savings, which would make resources available for more public or private investment.

This mechanism is one aspect of the alternative closure rules applied to the GEM by Dethier and Esfahani.[7] Basically they distinguish between a Keynesian closure rule, which yields the results already mentioned, and a neoclassical closure rule. For the neoclassical rule, they assume that the labor supply is fixed, and savings, which are mainly determined by government policy, are exogenous. Investment adjusts endogenously to savings with fixed sectoral shares. Under these assumptions they arrive at very different results for the macroeconomic effects of subsidies. In the absence of subsidies the price of food would increase and food demand would decline as under Keynesian assumptions. However, because food output would also decline, the released labor would be allocated to other sectors, and the output of the rest of the economy would increase. Due to increased government savings, investment would also increase, and as a net effect the reduction of subsidies would have positive growth implications for the overall economy. In other words, subsidies cannot be said to favor economic growth if aggregate demand can also be maintained without subsidies.

One way to increase aggregate demand when subsidies are reduced is through a wage-price spiral: if food prices went up there would be pressure to increase wages. The resulting wage increments would be passed on in further price increases, which would again cause wages to increase, which would generate additional demand. Another way of increasing aggregate demand would be to create additional public demand in the form of public current consumption or public investment. Taylor demonstrates with a Keynesian model that with both a wage-price spiral and increased investment to maintain aggregate demand, income distribution might be further biased toward the urban population.[8] Yet in the short run the absorptive capacity of the economy might not allow for a full substitution of investment spending for subsidy expenditures.

So a reduction or a removal of subsidies would not automatically have contractive effects on the economy. Alternative model formulations show a wide range of outcomes and related policy scenarios.

However, a major weakness of the GEM, at least in its current state, is the lack of flexibility on the supply side.[9] Domestic supply is modeled with Cobb-Douglas value-added functions and reacts only to changes in demand. This implies that a price-induced reduction of demand causes domestic supply to fall as well, without taking into account

---

[6] See Henry J. Bruton, "Four Issues of Economic Policy in Egypt," Economic Studies Unit, Ministry of Economy, Foreign Trade and Economic Cooperation, Cairo, 1980 (mimeographed).

[7] Dethier and Esfahani, "Macro-effects of Alternative Price Policies."

[8] See Taylor, "Food Subsidies in Egypt."

[9] See Richard S. Eckaus, F. D. McCarthy, and A. Mohie el-Din, "Multi-Sector General Equilibrium Policy Models for Egypt," Development Research and Technology Planning Centre, Cairo University, 1979 (mimeographed), pp. 8-16; and Eckaus and Mohie el-Din, "Consequences of Changes in Food Subsidy Policies," pp. 16-17.

separate producer price movements. This weakness obviously comes from the treatment of trade in the model. This may not matter as long as the model is used for short-term policy analysis, but it has important implications when the long-run effects of food subsidies on the agricultural sector are to be represented.

Theoretically, agriculture could gain from the subsidy-induced increase in food demand, depending on agriculture's competitiveness with imports and on practical policies. Under the prevailing conditions in Egypt, the additional demand is largely met with foreign goods. Hence, it is likely that agriculture does not gain and that the price disincentive effect has dominated in the past.

The models now available do not allow a full empirical test of these hypothetical implications. Taking the GEM as an example, the following aspects limit its applicability to specific agricultural questions.

1. Although imports of consumer goods are not considered to be competitive with domestic goods, in reality most of them are, especially wheat, meat, and sugar. Therefore, domestic supply mainly responds to demand and not to economic indicators.

2. Although the Egyptian government operates its food policy with procurement and price policies, such instruments are not included in the model.

3. The model only deals with the price effects of subsidies on consumer demand where prices are computed as markups of production costs, indirect taxes, and subsidies. As Eckaus and Mohie el-Din point out, the existence of rationing may yield very different conclusions, depending on whether subsidies are affected by a change in the amount of a subsidized commodity or by changes in the subsidy rates.[10]

4. The GEM identifies four agricultural production sectors. These are not quite enough for an analysis of product-specific subsidies. The staple food group, for instance, includes wheat, which is not rationed and which is mostly imported, and rice, which is rationed and is controlled through a strict procurement policy. For maize, which is in the same group, increasing amounts of

imports are released at subsidized prices for use as livestock feed. An aggregate model can hardly be used to examine the impact of these subsidies, nor can it be used to assess the influence of subsidies on the costs of meat and milk production.

5. Available applications of the GEM indicate that distributional effects vary widely, depending on the assumptions made for the subsidy and the macroeconomic closure rule. Subsidies generally seem to increase the net progressiveness of the fiscal system. Yet the results of the GEM applications by Dethier and Esfahani indicate that the distribution within sectors is quite stable, whereas the distribution between the rural and the urban sectors reacts more sensitively to changes in the assumptions about the closure rules.[11] Eckaus and Mohie el-Din show that subsidy effects are progressive only when subsidies are made effective by a decline in prices. For instance, if a subsidy is reduced as the result of a reduction in the quantity of subsidized imports and not as a result of a reduction of subsidy rates, the Eckaus and Mohie el-Din model shows a shift in the distribution of income in favor of agriculture.[12]

6. Finally, one must realize that some of the allocational implications of subsidies will be dynamic rather than static as the typical GEM assumes. This is true not only of the growth effects, the effects that could be expected from higher shares of investment in total aggregate demand as a consequence of reduced subsidies. Even if investment were stable and subsidies reduced current public expenditure on other items, such as agricultural research and extension, it is likely that such budget reallocations would inhibit the growth of agricultural production, which the available models would not cover. Unfortunately, there has so far been little empirical research on the productivity effects of alternative agricultural development plans and related budget appropriations.

For the purposes of this study, the lack of an endogenous domestic supply response module is probably the most critical problem with these models. Price increases from a cut in subsidies may not only reduce demand, as the models indicate, but they may

---

[10] Eckaus and Mohie el-Din, "Consequences of Changes in Food Subsidy Policies," pp. 37-54.

[11] Dethier and Esfahani, "Macro-effects of Alternative Price Policies."

[12] Eckaus and Mohie el-Din, "Consequences of Changes in Food Subsidy Policies," pp. 42-55.

also cause the share of domestic production in total supplies to increase. Moreover, even with a given subsidy, several policy systems can separate producer prices from the consumer markets. In fact, many dual price policy systems are being used in the Egyptian agricultural markets.

A more recent modeling approach, the Domestic Resource Mobilization Model (DRM), does provide the possibility of modeling the domestic supply response, at least indirectly.[13] As in the GEM, subsidy variations have a price and an income effect on demand where the changes in demand are governed by a linear expenditure system. The demand for imported goods is then derived from total demand and the relative prices of domestic and imported goods. Although this could make it easier to study the production effects of subsidies, the DRM does not treat the production of agricultural commodities as endogenous. Wheat production is exogenous in the model and cotton is realistically treated as a specific export commodity. Cotton exports, however, are related to aggregate cotton production simply by a growth elasticity.

The DRM is more flexible than the GEM on macroeconomic closure rules. It can also produce time paths of development. Although total domestic production is governed by the demand module, which includes import substitution, domestic resource use and resource capacities are adjusted as functions of technical progress, population growth, intersectoral migration, and capital accumulation. Capital accumulation is determined exogenously by specific investment policies.

The DRM was used to analyze the effects of a reduction in food subsidies. Specifically, a reduction in wheat subsidies, an increase in the domestic wheat price, and a complete removal of all other subsidies were examined. The positive macroeconomic effects dominated the solution as in the neoclassical version of the GEM. The foreign exchange gap and the savings gap narrowed. Agricultural exports increased, whereas the commodity composition of imports shifted toward nonagricultural imports, which was mainly a reaction to a positive effect on agricultural incomes.

In sum, three tentative conclusions can be drawn from these macroeconomic models. First, subsidies do not automatically support or impair economic growth. That depends on the accompanying government policies. Second, subsidies contribute to the progressiveness of the fiscal system. In other words, low-income households benefit more than high-income households. Third, macroeconomic models can only give results for overall economic activities, of which agriculture is a part. Implications for agriculture must be derived from these.

The research reviewed in this chapter has focused on quantitative models. The complex structure of Egypt's agriculture and the evolution of its agricultural policy and rural development strategies is not explained by these models, but must be taken as given. A complete assessment of these issues is beyond the scope of this study.[14]

Finally, this study does not evaluate the effect of food price and subsidy policies on the distribution of personal income in agriculture. These issues are dealt with elsewhere.[15]

---

[13] World Bank, *Arab Republic of Egypt: Domestic Resource Mobilization.*

[14] See Mahmoud Abdel-Fadil, *Development, Income Distribution and Social Change in Rural Egypt (1952-1970),* Department of Applied Economics, Occasional Paper 45 (Cambridge: Cambridge University Press, 1975); and Alan Richards, *Egypt's Agricultural Development, 1800-1980: Technical and Social Change* (Boulder, Colo.: Westview Press, 1982).

[15] See Alderman, von Braun, and Sakr, *Egypt's Food Subsidy and Rationing System.*

3

THE ECONOMIC DEVELOPMENT OF AGRICULTURE AND POLICY FORMATION

To analyze the effects of food prices and subsidies on agriculture, an understanding of Egypt's agricultural system during the 1960s and 1970s is needed.

The Role of Agriculture in the Economy

In 1980 agriculture contributed about 20 percent to the total GDP but employed about 40 percent of the work force. Although agriculture is the largest employer, the two figures highlight a strong intersectoral income disparity (Table 1). Disproportionately low investment may be one reason why the annual growth rate of agriculture was as low as 2 percent per year during the 1960s and 1970s. In the 1970s exceptionally high growth of the nonagricultural sectors, particularly petroleum, caused agriculture's share of GDP to drop 3 percent per year. But its share of employment has been shrinking at roughly the same rate (3.5 percent per year), leaving a high intersectoral income gap.[16] Despite the high migration of farm labor into other sectors, to urban centers, and even to other countries, particularly the Gulf States, the total labor force in agriculture remained more or less constant during the 1970s. About 3.9 million people were employed in agriculture in 1965/66, 4.1 million in 1970/71, and 4.2 million in 1979/80.[17]

For centuries agriculture was Egypt's major source of foreign exchange earnings. Cotton policy and its coordination with wheat production and import policies dominated the country's foreign exchange and food policies until the 1970s.[18] But agriculture's share of all goods exported dropped from 80 percent to 16 percent during the period 1970-80. At the same time the share of food imports in all imports increased from 21 percent to 34 percent. If factor and nonfactor services are included, agriculture's share of all goods exported was only about 8 percent in 1980 and food was 26 percent of all goods imported.[19] Although the value of agricultural exports in the 1960s and early 1970s was more than twice as high as the value of food imports, in 1980 only about 29 percent of the food import bill was paid by agricultural exports.

Not only did the share of agricultural exports in total exports decline, but the absolute amount of agricultural exports dropped by nearly one half between 1970 and 1980. Demand grew far faster than agriculture, as the rapidly shrinking degree of self-sufficiency in almost all food commodities indicates. Self-sufficiency in cereals declined from 83 percent in 1970/71 to 60 percent in 1980.

---

[16] For a detailed discussion of agricultural-nonagricultural income distribution see Ibrahim el-Issawy, "Interconnections Between Income Distribution and Economic Growth in the Context of Egypt's Economic Development," in *The Political Economy of Income Distribution in Egypt*, ed. Gouda Abdel-Khalek and Robert L. Tignor (New York: Holmes and Meier, 1981), pp. 96-98.

[17] Labor force statistics are not consistent. Hansen and Radwan report an annual rate of change of –1.4 percent between 1971 and 1979 based on labor force surveys of the Central Agency for Public Mobilization and Statistics. See Bent Hansen and Samir Radwan, *Employment Opportunities and Equity in a Changing Economy: Egypt in the 1980s* (Geneva: International Labour Office, 1982), pp. 59-60; Egypt, Central Agency for Public Mobilization and Statistics, *Population and Development* (Cairo: CAPMAS, 1978), pp. 226-227; and Central Agency for Public Mobilization and Statistics, *Statistical Yearbook of Egypt* (Cairo: CAPMAS, 1980), p. 226.

[18] An extensive analysis of this policy is provided in Richards, *Egypt's Agricultural Development.*

[19] Egypt, Ministry of Economy, "Egypt: Macroeconomic Performance, Problems and Prospects," Cairo, 1981 (mimeographed), Tables 5 and 6; Egypt, Ministry of Agriculture and the U.S. Agency for International Development, *Strategies for Accelerating Agricultural Development* (Cairo: Ministry of Agriculture/USAID, 1982), p. 74; Egypt, Ministry of Agriculture, Institute of Agricultural Economics, Research, and Statistics, "Production Statistics," Cairo, 1982 (mimeographed); and Egypt, Ministry of Supply and Home Trade, "Trade Statistics," Cairo, 1982 (mimeographed).

Table 1—Share of agriculture in the economy, various years

	1965/66	1970/71	1979/80
	(percent)		
Share of total GDP[a]	28.4	27.5	21.0
Share of total gross fixed investment	8.1	7.8	8.0[b]
Share of total employment	53.4	53.2	39.3[b]

Sources: Egypt, Central Agency for Public Mobilization and Statistics, *Statistical Yearbook of Egypt* (Cairo: CAPMAS, 1980), pp. 222-227; Egypt, Ministry of Economy, "Egypt: Macroeconomic Performance, Problems and Prospects," Cairo, 1981 (mimeographed), Tables 5 and 6; and World Bank, *Arab Republic of Egypt: Economic Management in a Period of Transition* (Washington, D.C.: World Bank, 1978), 6:11.

[a] The figures for gross domestic product (GDP) are at current prices.

[b] This figure is for 1979.

The food security issue is extensively discussed in Egypt mainly with respect to this reduction in self-sufficiency.[20] A wider view of the food security issue focuses on the decreased ability of agriculture to provide the means to compensate for the growing food import bill.[21]

While the first viewpoint merely leads to a strategy stressing domestic provision of cereals, the second asks for a balancing of the foreign exchange budget between sectors. Both strategies might have some rationale on political grounds, but both can reduce economic efficiency. A sector modeling exercise concludes that to increase cereal production as much as desired, cereals would have to be highly protected. Balancing the sectoral foreign exchange budget would, on the other hand, require protection of the sector as a whole, if current per capita consumption is to be maintained.[22]

Farm Structures, Resources, and the Land Use Pattern

There are about 3.5 million farms in Egypt, with an average size of 1.6 feddans.[23] In 1977, 52 percent of farm land belonged to farms smaller than 5 feddans, which made up 95 percent of all holdings (Table 2). Furthermore, about 40 percent of all farms are less than 1 feddan; these constitute just 12 percent of the total area.[24] The pressure of a growing population in combination with the customs for inheritance of land have led to an increase in the number of holdings, which has increased the man-land ratio and rural poverty.[25]

The amount of arable land is a major constraint to increasing agricultural production. About 5.8 million feddans of fully irrigated "old" lands and 0.5 million feddans of newly reclaimed desert land were under cultivation in 1980. These 6.3 million feddans cover about 3 percent of the total land area of Egypt. This land, along the Nile and in the Nile Delta, has some of the best soil in the world and is perennially irrigated. Rainfed agriculture is insignificant. Expanding arable land has been economically, technically, and managerially difficult.[26]

The water supply for year-round agricultural production, which Egypt's weather conditions make possible, is regulated at the Aswan High Dam. This gives Egyptian

---

[20] The issue is given major attention in Egypt, Ministry of Agriculture and the U.S. Agency for International Development, *Strategies for Accelerating Agricultural Development.*

[21] An analysis of the food security issue is provided by Ahmed Goueli, "Food Security Program in Egypt," in *Food Security for Developing Countries,* ed. Alberto Valdés (Boulder, Colo.: Westview Press, 1981), pp. 143-157.

[22] See Joachim von Braun and Hartwig de Haen, "Egypt and the Enlargement of the EEC: Impact on the Agricultural Sector," *Food Policy* 7 (February 1982): 46-56.

[23] A feddan equals 1.038 acres.

[24] See Richard Adams, "Growth Without Development in Rural Egypt: A Local-level Study of Institutional and Social Change," Ph.D. thesis, University of California, Berkeley, 1981, p. 25.

[25] Samir Radwan and Eddy Lee, "The Anatomy of Rural Poverty, Egypt 1977," World Employment Programme, Geneva, 1980 (mimeographed).

[26] Carl H. Gotsch and Wayne M. Dyer, "Rhetoric and Reason in the Egyptian 'New Lands' Debate," *Food Research Institute Studies* 18 (No. 2, 1982): 129-148.

Table 2—Area and holdings, by farm size, 1952, 1961, and 1977

Farm Size, Holdings	Area			Holdings		
	1952	1961	1977	1952	1961	1977
Less than 5 feddans (percent)	35.4	52.1	52.0	94.3	94.1	95.0
5 – 20 feddans (percent)	19.5	19.1	21.4	4.5	4.7	4.0
More than 20 feddans (percent)	45.1	28.8	26.6	1.2	1.2	1.0
Average size (feddans)	2.1	2.0	1.6	...	...	...
Number of holdings (1,000)	...	...	...	2,801	3,101	3,462

Source: Egypt, Central Agency for Public Mobilization and Statistics, *Statistical Yearbook of Egypt* (Cairo: CAPMAS, 1980), pp. 54-56.

agriculture the characteristics of a huge irrigation project. Total water supply may increase during the next decades due to changes in the southern Nile system. But the total supply of irrigation water seems to be less a constraint than its management.[27]

A complex system of overlapping rotations is characteristic of Egypt's agriculture. Figure 2 describes the cropping pattern in 1977-79. The cropping intensity averages about 190, whereas it was 176 in the early 1960s. With a higher share of vegetable crops, shortened growing periods for new varieties of staple crops, and decreased fallow it might well exceed 200 in the future.[28]

Development of Production Structures and Economic Incentives

Agricultural production structures changed remarkably during the 1960s and 1970s. In the early 1960s the completion of the Aswan High Dam caused land use patterns and cropping intensities to change. The process of adjusting to the new water availability continued until the second half of the 1960s. Since then changing economic incentives and direct government intervention in allocation have been mainly responsible for shifting land use patterns and growth of livestock production.

Among the winter crops, the fodder area, which is devoted to a full-season clover called berseem, changed the most, growing from about 1.2 million feddans in 1965 to 1.7 million feddans in 1980. Among the summer crops, cotton showed the largest reduction, while wheat area remained more or less constant. The increase in full-season berseem area was primarily at the cost of the area for pulses and short-season berseem, which are cultivated before cotton. Total land area has increased 2-300,000 feddans since the mid-1960s, which has allowed the area used for fruit and vegetable crops to expand.[29]

The land use pattern in the summer season shows a continuous growth of maize area and a reduction of cotton and sorghum cultivation.[30] Maize area increased by 30 percent (about 0.5 million feddans) and cotton area shrank by 35 percent (0.7 million feddans) between 1965 and 1980. The rice area remained almost constant at about 1.1 million feddans during the 1970s.

The tremendous expansion of fodder and animal feed production in both seasons—berseem in winter and maize in summer—reflects the growing livestock herd. The

---

[27] John Waterbury, *Hydropolitics of the Nile Valley* (Syracuse, N.Y.: Syracuse University Press, 1979).

[28] James B. Fitch and Afaf A. Aziz, "Multiple Cropping Intensity in Egyptian Agriculture: A Study of its Determinants," Research Paper 5, Microeconomic Study of the Egyptian Farm System, Ministry of Agriculture, Cairo, October 1980.

[29] No accurate data on total land are available, as new land under cultivation and losses of cultivated land for non-agricultural purposes are only roughly estimated.

[30] The *nili* season (autumn) is included in the summer season.

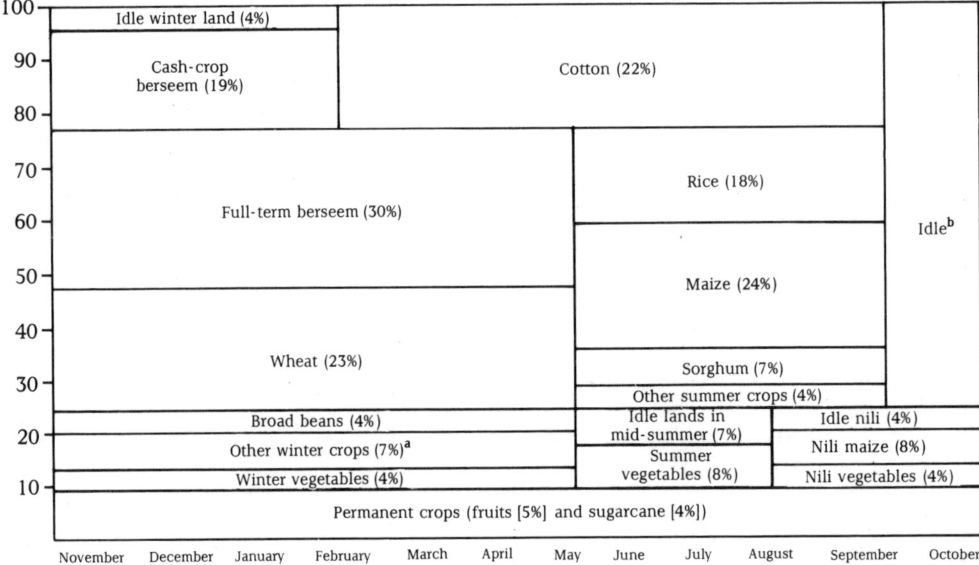

Figure 2—Cropping pattern, 1977-79

Source: Nabil T. Habashi, James B. Fitch, and Salwa Rehiwi, "Egypt's Agricultural Cropping Pattern, A Review of the System by which it is Managed and its Relationship to Price Policy," Research Paper No. 4, Microeconomic Study of the Egyptian Farm System, Ministry of Agriculture, Cairo, November 1980, p. 2.

[a] Includes lentils, chick peas, fenugreek, flax, barley, and other crops.

[b] Represents land that is temporarily idle between summer crops, such as cotton and rice, and winter crops, such as berseem.

number of cattle, buffalo, sheep, and goats has increased 30-50 percent since the mid-1960s.

The changes in net returns per feddan of the major crops reveal that the dynamic reallocation of crops corresponds to the comparative advantages of the rotations. In 8 out of the 16 years from 1965 to 1980 the berseem-maize rotation provided the highest return to land. In 5 years returns of the berseem-rice rotation exceeded it slightly and in 3 years during the late 1960s and early 1970s the short-season berseem-cotton rotation was highest (Appendix 1, Tables 30 and 31). Since the late 1960s the profitability of fodder crops has increased far more rapidly than the profitability of cotton. This explains the major shift in crop allocation. The ratios of the net returns of rice and maize and of wheat and full-season berseem have not changed as much. The relative stability of the area of these cereals is partly determined by the importance of wheat as a subsistence crop and wheat straw as fodder. Government control of the area allotment of rice has had an effect as well.

Agricultural Policy Goals and Instruments

Egypt's agricultural policy is best understood as having two goals. The first is to provide adequate basic foods to all groups of the population, including those with low incomes. The second goal is for Egypt to become fully self-sufficient in as many food commodities as possible. Since the revolution of 1952, two political factors have helped to determine these goals: the security of social peace and stability, on the one hand, and external independence, on the other hand.

More specifically, the goals of agricultural policy during the past 15 years have been to stabilize farm prices, to procure basic food commodities, to increase productivity, to increase public revenue, and to improve the balance of payments.[31]

The goal of price stability became important during the 1970s when world market prices of most agricultural commodities fluctuated greatly, peaking in 1973/74 and 1979/80. Procurement prices and average producer prices rose rapidly during this time. Riots in January 1977, which followed an attempt to increase prices of subsidized consumer goods, reinforced the belief that keeping prices stable was of prime importance.

Since Egypt has enjoyed relatively peaceful foreign relations, foreign exchange availability has increased due to growing oil exports, Suez Canal revenues, and remittances from Egyptian workers in Arab countries. There are indications that these improvements favor a closer orientation of domestic agricultural prices to the trends of international prices. Whether these trends have

indeed caused the emphasis on the budget and foreign exchange to be reduced remains to be analyzed. A large number of programs to increase the productivity of specific crops, such as maize, rice, and beans, have been initiated, and irrigation and drainage programs have been undertaken. Even though the total supply of basic food commodities, which had been repeatedly disturbed during political crises and the wars of 1967 and 1973, has markedly increased, a rising proportion of this supply comes from imports, and the self-sufficiency of major food items has declined considerably (Table 3).

The Egyptian government has, for a long time, directly influenced the performance of agriculture by investing in land reclamation and irrigation, by controlling input supplies, and by keeping strict control in general of private farming. Several of these policies are related to food subsidies. These include area allotment, procurement, direct and indirect price controls for agricultural

Table 3—Self-sufficiency of major agricultural commodities, 1965-80

Year	Wheat	Maize	Rice	Lentils	Beans	Sugar	Cotton Lint	Red Meat
1965	0.35	0.93	1.37	0.93	1.00	0.99	2.34	0.81
1966	0.40	0.93	1.41	0.95	1.00	0.69	3.28	0.84
1967	0.31	0.91	1.41	0.73	1.00	0.79	2.61	0.92
1968	0.40	0.94	1.51	0.73	1.00	1.07	2.22	0.93
1969	0.31	0.96	1.88	0.56	1.00	1.17	1.74	0.93
1970	0.37	0.97	1.64	0.64	1.00	1.17	2.05	0.89
1971	0.38	0.98	1.42	0.89	0.90	1.26	2.47	0.87
1972	0.37	0.96	1.37	0.83	0.97	0.99	2.09	0.89
1973	0.36	0.97	1.25	0.82	1.00	1.11	2.18	0.88
1974	0.34	0.87	1.10	0.79	0.91	0.91	2.00	0.82
1975	0.34	0.86	1.07	0.42	0.67	0.81	1.83	0.87
1976	0.34	0.86	1.16	0.35	0.75	0.80	1.66	0.75
1977	0.27	0.82	1.18	0.32	0.91	0.84	1.52	0.81
1978	0.25	0.81	1.10	0.24	0.92	0.74	1.45	0.75
1979	0.27	0.85	1.12	0.13	0.87	0.80	1.47	0.79
1980	0.24	0.77	1.07	0.10	0.85	0.65	1.42	0.75

Sources: Computed from data provided by the Egyptian Ministry of Agriculture and the Central Agency for Public Mobilization and Statistics.

Notes: Self-sufficiency coefficient equals domestic production divided by total domestic use. Total domestic use equals production plus imports minus exports. Where foreign trade includes processed goods (sugar and cotton lint), the raw material equivalents of traded quantities are used.

---

[31] On agricultural development objectives and policy, see Youssef Wally, *Strategy for Agricultural Development in the Eighties for the Arab Republic of Egypt*, International Development Series Report No. 9 (Ames, Iowa: Iowa State University, 1982), pp. 58-63.

commodities, and input pricing and allotment.

Area Allotment

There are several reasons why the Egyptian government allocates areas for specific crops, even at the farm level.[32] In the past, area was allotted partly to prevent overproduction of crops such as cotton and rice. During the 1960s and 1970s the instrument was used to enforce production of minimum amounts of politically desired crops. Today, a prominent objective is to ensure that certain amounts of food commodities are produced domestically. Another objective is to ensure that production of export crops, mainly cotton and rice, is large enough to reach foreign exchange targets in spite of low fixed producer prices. At least this was a purpose until foreign exchange became available from other sources in the second half of the 1970s. Area allotments also help to assure that crop production is on a large enough scale to facilitate efficient operation of irrigation and pesticide programs.

Although area allotments undoubtedly have a significant effect on the pattern of production, there is evidence that farmers often illegally deviate from prescribed area allotments when they can get higher income from an alternative area allocation. Table 4 indicates that the actual area for all crops for which the plan is enforced—rice, beans, lentils, and cotton—is lower than the planned area. The area planning for the remaining crops only indicates what is desired and is not enforced. However, the more or less enforced area allocations for rice and cotton in the summer season have strong repercussions on the whole cropping system, given the interseasonal effects of cotton in the rotation scheme (see Figure 2). The interdependency of area allotment by the government and decisions on allocations by farmers will be discussed later.

Procurement

As indicated earlier, the government operates a system of compulsory deliveries

Table 4—Government area planning and actual area for various crops, 1979-80

Crop	Planned	Actual	Enforced or Not
	(1,000 feddans)		
Wheat	1,380	1,391	Not enforced
Rice	1,100	1,039	Enforced
Maize	1,761	1,884	Not enforced
Beans	300	287	Enforced
Lentils	40	22	Enforced
Sugarcane	290	249	Not enforced[a]
Onions (winter)	36	22	Not enforced[a]
Garlic	23	16	Not enforced[a]
Cotton	1,301	1,196	Enforced

Source: Data provided by the Egyptian Ministry of Agriculture.

[a] For these crops contractual agreements are settled with farmers in certain regions. They involve delivery of the crop at a fixed price.

at fixed prices. The entire cotton crop and a high share of the winter onion crop must be sold to the cooperatives at low prices. Among the basic food commodities certain proportions of wheat, rice, beans, lentils, sesame, and groundnuts are subject to the quota system. In the case of sugarcane, nearly all of the crop is sold to the government because all of the processing facilities are state owned.

The shares of total production that are procured at low prices vary among commodities and in time (Table 5). Rice has the largest volume of procurement, usually amounting to one half of total production. Traditionally a major portion of this was exported, but the amount that is distributed domestically has steadily increased. Wheat, the second most important procurement food crop, has had a significantly lower relative quota of 15-20 percent. Moreover, the quota dropped drastically in 1977, when forced deliveries officially ceased. Actually, some procurement continued even after

---

[32] See Nabil T. Habashi, James B. Fitch, and Salwi Rehiwi, "Egypt's Agricultural Cropping Pattern: A Review of the System by which it is Managed and its Relationship to Price Policy," Research Paper 4, Microeconomic Study of the Egyptian Farm System, Ministry of Agriculture, Cairo, November 1980.

Table 5—Procurement of major food commodities as a percentage of total production, 1965-80

Year	Wheat[a]	Rice	Beans[b]	Lentils[b]
		(percent)		
1965	18.0	50.0	...	...
1966	17.6	50.0	...	...
1967	19.2	50.8	...	...
1968	18.6	51.1	...	...
1969	10.6	52.4	...	...
1970	12.0	44.3	5.0	...
1971	16.5	42.1	33.9	...
1972	14.9	40.6	21.9	...
1973	15.3	40.7	11.6	...
1974	19.0	38.6	15.3	...
1975	18.7	48.0	21.8	20.2
1976	15.3	47.2	25.0	40.7
1977	8.1	46.3	22.5	65.8
1978	6.5	47.0	18.2	38.1
1979	15.5	51.9	34.4	91.1
1980	6.9	51.2	31.7	64.2

Sources: Data on procurement of wheat, beans, and lentils were compiled from unpublished data provided by the Principal Bank for Development and Agricultural Investment, 1982; and data on procurement of rice and production of wheat, beans, lentils, and rice were obtained from the Egyptian Ministry of Agriculture, 1982.

[a] Wheat procurement for 1965-68 is a rough estimate by the Principal Bank for Development and Agricultural Investment; no actual data were available.

[b] It could not be fully ascertained whether beans were procured during 1965-69 or whether lentils were procured during 1965-74. Ahmed Hassan in a recent publication mentions 1967 as the year of introduction of delivery quotas for beans and lentils (Ahmed Hassan, "Cooperative Marketing and Compulsory Deliveries of Some Agricultural Crops," Institute of National Planning, Cairo, 1982 [mimeographed]).

1977, apparently as a result of local arrangements and special regulations for farms on area distributed during the land reform of the 1960s. In 1979 as much wheat was procured as during the period of enforced deliveries. Other procurement crops, like beans and lentils, are procured in much smaller quantities, but relative shares have been significant in recent years.

The declared purpose of wheat procurement has traditionally been to ensure a stable flow of domestic grain to the urban population. But the factors that apparently motivated the drastic reduction of wheat procurement in 1977 suggest that the budget is an important constraint for the achievement of this goal. In the past, procurement prices were close to import prices (converted at official exchange rates). When world market prices went up during the world food crisis (1973/74), consumer prices were kept well below import prices. The consequence was a heavy burden on the subsidy budget for wheat imports. This may explain why procurement quotas were raised and enforced with vigor during that period, at prices that increased much more slowly than world prices. By 1975 the situation changed. Import prices declined again, while procurement prices, being more or less strictly linked to costs of production and inflation, continued to grow. The government reacted by drastically reducing domestic purchases and increasing the share of imports in urban supplies.

A model that regresses the relative quota of wheat procurement (w) on government revenues (r) and the ratio of procurement prices to import prices (p) supports the hypothesis that procurement is significantly influenced by the government's finances:

$$w = 31.03 - 9.46\,p - 0.0049\,r;$$
$$(-2.97)\ \ (-4.84)$$

$$\bar{R}^2 = 0.65,$$

where

w = the share of procurement in the production of wheat,

p = the share of the procurement price in the import price, at the official exchange rate, and

r = government revenues in LE million, deflated by the consumer price index.[33]

The time series is for the period 1965-80; t-values are in parentheses.

De Janvry, Siam, and Gad address themselves to the more general question of whether

---

[33] The Egyptian pound (LE) equals 100 piasters. In July 1982 US $1.22 equalled LE 1.00. Between 1977 and August 1981 the Egyptian pound equalled US $1.43. Prior to devaluation in 1977 the Egyptian pound was valued at more than $2.50.

forced deliveries are needed to ensure a sufficiently high market supply.[34] Their empirical case study for wheat and rice, based on predetermined elasticities of supply and demand, concludes that forced deliveries are irrelevant to food security in Egypt. Voluntary sales would increase more than proportionately if compulsory deliveries were halted. Moreover, the authors suggest that the dominant effect of this policy instrument is to tax farm incomes. The conclusion that it is irrelevant to ensure domestic supplies to urban areas comes from the assumption that the elasticities of supply with respect to changes of price are low for wheat and rice and that free sales are reduced by the quotas. In other words, a reduction of free sales reduces the immediate supply-increasing effect of the procurement policy. One side effect of this is that prices increase on the free markets, which reduces the welfare of those rural households that do not have full access to subsidized food markets and that produce less than their subsistence requirements.

Whether the results that de Janvry, Siam, and Gad obtained for 1976 with data taken from a sample of farms represent the sectoral aggregate and are valid for longer periods of time is unclear. But because the elasticities used lie within the range of the few available estimates, and because the gaps between procurement and the open market prices assumed for 1976 were not atypical for the 1960s and 1970s, the calculation appears to be reasonable.

Direct and Indirect Price Controls

The Egyptian government operates a complex set of market interventions and price regulations that not only cause domestic prices and price ratios of agricultural products to diverge from international prices but also cause differences in prices between more or less separated domestic markets even for the same commodity.[35] It is evident that these price distortions may affect the allocation of resources and production, consumption patterns, and foreign trade.

Egypt, like most other developing countries, tends to overvalue its currency. Most agricultural trade and several nonagricultural imports have been handled at the official foreign exchange rate. Other imports are subject to mixed financing, with a fixed share of foreign exchange converted at the official exchange rate and the rest at a higher, so-called parallel rate.[36] Finally, imports of some commodities must rely completely on foreign exchange from black market sources. When there is a quota on international trade and an increase in prosecutions on black market foreign exchange transactions, as in the 1960s, the black market rate is a somewhat distorted indicator of the marginal shadow price of foreign exchange. It is still used here for an assessment of price policy because there is no comprehensive model of the Egyptian foreign exchange market. The Egyptian government has devalued the Egyptian pound several times. Nevertheless, a comparison of official exchange rates with the black market rates for the dollar reveals a permanent, though fluctuating, overvaluation of the currency (see Table 6). This divergency of exchange rates makes export and import prices in Egyptian pounds appear to be lower than Egypt's international purchasing power.

The statistics of agricultural producer and consumer prices are incomplete in Egypt. Although fixed prices for producers and consumers are well documented, open market prices are generally not well known. Basically the open market prices used in this report are derived from unpublished statistics made available by the Central Agency for Public Mobilization and Statistics on free rural and urban consumer prices.[37] For wheat and pulses, free producer prices are assumed to be below free rural consumer

---

[34] Alain de Janvry, Gamal Siam, and Osman Gad, "Forced Deliveries: Their Impact on the Marketed Surplus and the Distribution of Income in Egyptian Agriculture," Economics Working Paper 38, Agricultural Development Systems Project, Ministry of Agriculture, Cairo, and the University of California-Berkeley, Cairo, September 1981.

[35] For a description of how price policies are implemented in Egypt, see William Cuddihy, *Agricultural Price Management in Egypt*, World Bank Staff Working Paper 388 (Washington, D.C.: World Bank, 1980).

[36] For more details on foreign exchange and trade policies and the impact of food subsidies, see Scobie, *Food Subsidies in Egypt*.

[37] These basic data are available from the authors upon request.

24

Table 6—Official and black market exchange rates, 1965-80

Year	Official	Black Market	Relative Foreign Exchange Bias[a]
		(US $/LE)	
1965	2.30	1.12	1.053
1966	2.30	1.09	1.110
1967	2.30	1.16	0.982
1968	2.30	1.20	0.916
1969	2.30	1.10	1.090
1970	2.30	1.09	1.110
1971	2.30	1.20	0.916
1972	2.30	1.24	0.854
1973	2.56	1.48	0.729
1974	2.56	1.57	0.630
1975	2.56	1.41	0.815
1976	2.56	1.35	0.896
1977	2.56	1.39	0.841
1978	2.56	1.39	0.841
1979	1.43	1.33	0.075
1980	1.43	1.22	0.172

Sources: Official exchange rates were obtained from the Central Bank of Egypt; black market exchange rates were taken from *Pick's Currency Yearbook*, various issues (New York: Franz Pick Publishing Co., various years).

[a] The relative deviation (B) of the black market rate (W_b, in LE/US$) from the official rate (W_o, in LE/US$) $= W_o/W_b - 1$.

prices by a marketing margin of 5 percent. Free producer prices of rice are calculated by deducting processing costs from free consumer prices. For maize, sugarcane, cotton, and livestock products, average producer prices, derived from Ministry of Agriculture data, are assumed to apply to the total domestic supply. This assumption is made because a separation of producer markets either does not exist (for example, for domestic maize and cotton) or is quantitatively unimportant. The latter is also true for sugar, where the majority of produce is sold to sugarcane factories, and for livestock, where prices are officially fixed for those livestock products that have been produced using subsidized feed but where the fixed prices are seldom enforced.

An analysis of the price changes reveals some general characteristics and some commodity-specific phenomena (see Figure 3). A general impression is that official domestic prices, to both producers and consumers, are much more stable than the corresponding international prices. Domestic free prices, on the other hand, fluctuate substantially. Throughout the 15-year period the domestic prices of grain (wheat, rice, and maize) and of pulses (beans and lentils) have been lower than the corresponding border price equivalents; domestic wheat and rice prices have been even lower than the international prices at the official exchange rate (see Appendix 1, Tables 32-33). Depending on whether they are compared to fixed or to open market prices and omitting the world market price boom of the early 1970s, border price equivalents at the farm gate have been two to three times higher than the producer prices of wheat and rice.

Maize prices are mainly influenced by the subsidized release of imported maize, most of which is used for feed. Because the demand for feed has expanded rapidly, faster than the rapidly growing maize imports, open market prices have risen much more swiftly than fixed prices. Protection of livestock products has favored this development.

This protection increased throughout the second half of the 1970s. More recently, producer prices of beef, for example, have been 20 to 40 percent higher than their border price equivalents at farm gate. Imports were admitted after 1973, but limitations on foreign exchange at the official exchange rate and a complicated system of import license restrictions made private meat imports difficult. On the consumer side, the government has subsidized sales, supplied mainly from imports. Most of this is frozen beef. With the exception of a price jump early in the 1970s the subsidized consumer prices have been stable; since 1974 they have even been nominally constant. But because these sales are rationed, there exists a free market for beef, where prices are considerably higher. The free market prices were even higher than world market prices in the second half of the 1970s. Nominal protection of milk products is also high, although a comparison of international and national prices is more difficult because the traded good, milk powder, cannot be easily compared to domestic milk products.

Input Subsidies

To assess the effects of price interventions on agricultural production, it is not enough to study the taxation of major field

Figure 3—Nominal protection coefficients of producer prices, 1965-80

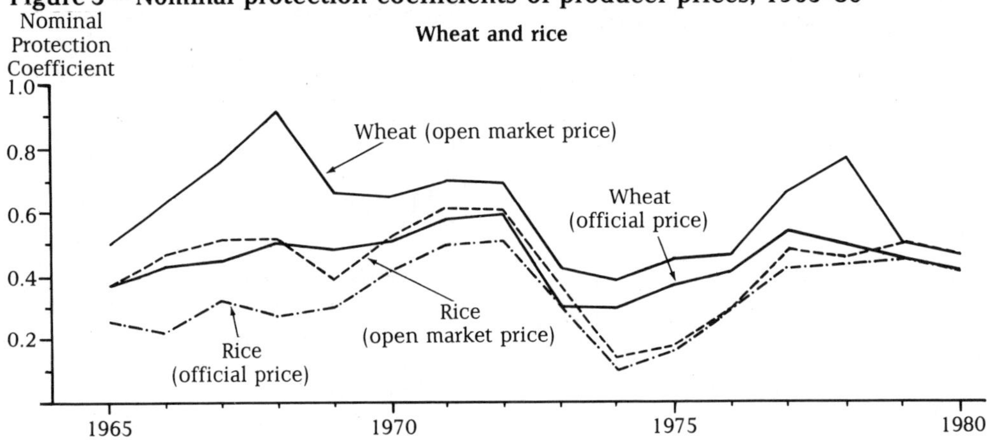

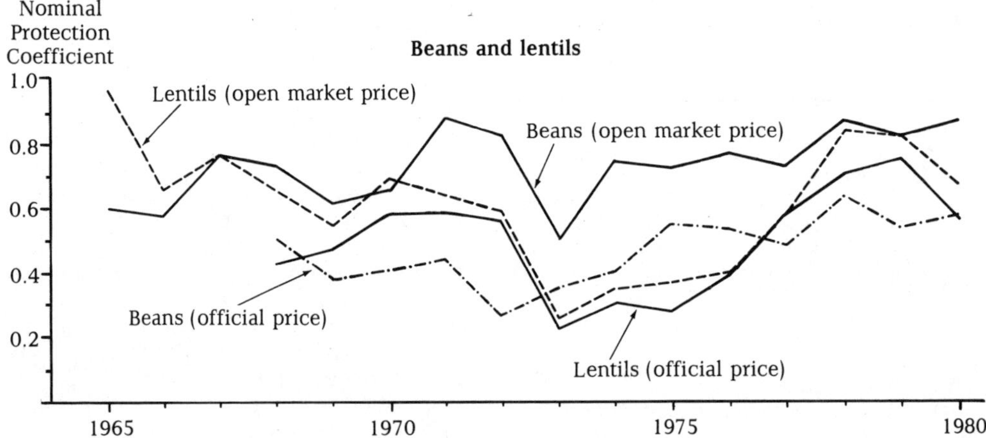

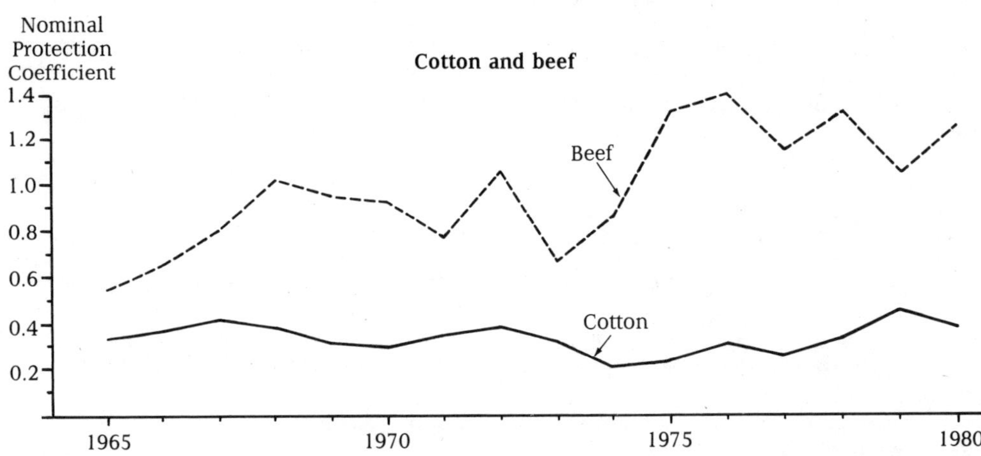

Notes: Nominal protection at the official price is the ratio of the official producer's price to the world market price equivalent at the farm gate. Nominal protection at the open market price is the ratio of the open market producer's price to the world market price equivalent at the farm gate. The world market prices are converted using the shadow exchange rate (as given in Table 6).

crops or the protection of livestock products alone. Several inputs, including fertilizer, cotton pesticides, and feed, are also provided at distorted prices. Moreover, farmers benefit from indirect subsidies, such as low fuel prices, free irrigation water, and other infrastructural services. A considerable share of the direct input subsidies go to pest control for cotton.

Fertilizer subsidies became important only after 1975 when world market prices rose and domestic prices were kept unchanged. With the beginning of the world market boom, the agricultural stabilization fund in the government budget, which until then had resulted in a net taxation of inputs, became a source of increasing input subsidization. This effect is clearly indicated by the drastic expansion of the total value of direct input subsidies, both in nominal and in real terms (see Table 7).

Because the subsidies on major inputs are large, they can be assumed to have an important effect on production. Accurate information is hard to find, but an attempt is made in Table 7 to compare domestic prices and international price equivalents for nitrogen fertilizer, cattle feed supplied by public feed mix companies, and berseem. Components of the cattle feed mix are evaluated at their international prices. The international price of berseem is computed under the assumption that 10 tons of berseem are equivalent in nutritional value to 1 ton of straw and 1 ton of feed mix.[38]

A comparison of national and international input prices indicates that fertilizer was taxed until the mid-1970s and was heavily subsidized in the latter part of the 1970s. The tax on fertilizer was the dominant factor in the overall budget effects of input price interventions. This changed when the volume of feed being distributed at highly subsidized prices began to rise. As the data in Table 7 indicate, the official release price of feed mix has always been exceeded by the

international price equivalent. Moreover, because the international value of feed mix has been relatively high, the computed international price equivalent of berseem is clearly higher than the domestic farm-gate price of berseem. The domestic price of berseem is affected by two counteracting factors: its marginal return in the livestock sector, which is characterized by low physical output/input ratios, and the taxed price of competing field crops. This may explain why the domestic berseem price lies below the international equivalent value despite protection of meat.

Taxation

The direct taxes on agriculture are only marginal. A land tax is levied on all arable land on the basis of the annual rental value of the land. The rental value is assessed by the Central Administration about every 10 years. This official rental value grossly underestimates the actual rental value of land. The tax, based on this official rental value, is paid by the landowner annually. Its basic rate is 14 percent. Between 1953 and 1973 taxable landowners whose tax liability did not exceed LE 4 were exempt. After 1973 properties of less than 3 feddans became exempt. The land tax contributes less than 1 percent to total tax revenues and therefore is not included in the following analyses.[39]

Agriculture is indirectly taxed through export taxes. The nominal protection rates for cotton and rice—the two major export crops of the 1960s and 1970s—indicate this. The major reason why this taxation policy was adopted is its administrative and political feasibility. Korayem concludes in her analysis of the issue that "it is easier and more beneficial, politically and economically, to the government to tax farmers' income disguisedly by the price differential policy of the agricultural crops than to tax this income explicitly by a specific progressive income tax."[40]

---

[38] Both quantities, 10 tons of berseem and 1 ton of feed mix plus 1 ton of straw, are roughly equivalent in energy and protein. Yet, a full substitution is not feasible due to differences in digestibility and other dietary properties. For a more detailed discussion of the problem of treating berseem as a traded good, see J. C. Ingram and T. Moursi, "Treating Berseem as a Traded Good in the Calculation of Social Returns," Economics Working Paper 18, Agricultural Development Systems Project, Ministry of Agriculture, Cairo, and the University of California-Berkeley, Cairo, May 1981.

[39] M. Reda A. el-Edel, "Impact of Taxation on Income Distribution: An Exploratory Attempt to Estimate Tax Incidence in Egypt," in *The Political Economy of Income Distribution in Egypt,* ed. Gouda Abdel-Khalek and Robert L. Tignor (New York: Holmes and Meier, 1981), p. 135.

[40] Karima Korayem, "The Agricultural Output Pricing Policy and the Implicit Taxation of Agricultural Income," in *The Political Economy of Income Distribution in Egypt,* ed. Gouda Abdel-Khalek and Robert L. Tignor (New York: Holmes and Meier, 1981), p. 184.

Table 7—Agricultural input subsidies and distortion of selected agricultural input prices, 1965-80

Year	Nitrogen Domestic[a]	Nitrogen International Equivalent[b]	Feed Mix Official[c]	Feed Mix International Equivalent[d]	Berseem Producer Price	Berseem International Equivalent[e]	Total Input Subsidies Current Prices	Total Input Subsidies Deflated[f]
	(LE/metric ton)						(LE million)	
1965	145.0	131.0	12.5	79.3	3.7	8.0	−2.0	−3.1
1966	145.0	117.0	12.5	87.4	3.5	8.9	−1.0	−1.4
1967	145.0	103.0	12.5	79.6	3.4	8.1	−3.0	−4.2
1968	145.0	94.0	13.5	66.2	2.2	6.7	−6.0	−8.5
1969	145.0	83.0	13.5	73.3	2.6	7.5	−4.0	−5.5
1970	145.0	72.0	13.5	77.4	2.4	7.8	−3.0	−4.0
1971	145.0	77.0	13.5	73.8	2.8	7.5	−4.0	−5.1
1972	145.0	103.0	13.5	72.6	2.3	7.3	12.0	15.2
1973	145.0	138.0	13.5	76.9	4.3	7.9	13.0	15.8
1974	145.0	264.0	21.0	88.0	5.2	9.0	12.0	13.1
1975	145.0	356.0	21.0	78.9	4.8	8.2	81.0	81.0
1976	145.0	362.0	25.0	97.7	5.6	10.0	34.0	30.8
1977	145.0	370.0	25.0	106.7	7.0	11.2	35.0	28.1
1978	145.0	377.0	25.0	105.7	9.1	11.1	36.0	26.0
1979	155.0	384.0	30.0	104.2	8.7	11.0	50.0	98.8
1980	. . .	. . .	30.0	130.5	11.2	13.7	72.0	92.5

Sources: The prices of nitrogen in 1965-75 are from R. R. Newberg, "Fertilizer Subsector Assessment: Egypt," Multinational Agribusiness Systems, Washington, D.C, 1979 (mimeographed). The 1976-79 prices of nitrogen are from E. A. Zaglui, "Some Proposals to Reduce Agricultural Subsidies," Ministry of Agriculture Paper 6, Cairo, 1979 (mimeographed). The figures for feed mix and berseem are from unpublished data from the Egyptian Ministry of Agriculture, obtained in 1982. The total input subsidies in the government budget, in current prices, are from unpublished data obtained from the Egyptian Ministry of Finance.

[a] These are the average prices of nitrogen fertilizer.

[b] These are the import prices (c.i.f. at the official exchange rate) of ammonium sulfate plus the domestic costs of marketing and transportation.

[c] These figures are the prices of cattle feed mix for fattening.

[d] The international equivalent price of feed mix is calculated as the weighted sum of the international prices at the shadow exchange rate for cattle feed mix components, where the weights are equal to the time variant quantity shares.

[e] The international equivalent of 10 tons of berseem is calculated as the sum of the international equivalent value of 1 ton of cattle feed mix at the shadow exchange rate and the value of 1 ton of straw at domestic prices.

[f] These figures were deflated by the consumer price index (1975=100).

4

EFFECTS ON PRODUCTION OF AGRICULTURAL PRICE POLICIES AND GOVERNMENT INTERVENTION

Previous studies have demonstrated that Egyptian farmers, like most farmers, respond to changes in economic incentives, though empirical estimates of that response vary greatly.[41] Price responsiveness is evident in area allocation and crop yields, in the rapid reallocation of labor between farm and nonfarm employment, and in the international migration of farm labor.

Because of the complexity of technical conditions, such as the overlapping of seasons, and institutional constraints, such as area allotment and procurement, supply elasticities are not readily available or easily estimated for Egyptian agriculture. Econometric estimates of the supply response undertaken for this study were rejected because they were inconsistent on the aggregate sector level. Modeling the price responsiveness of yields seems to be even more difficult than modeling area response. Technical changes in farm production have been dramatic during the last two decades. Cuddihy was able to obtain statistically valid results with yield response models for the period 1950-75, but an attempt in this research to estimate crop-specific models for a more recent time period, 1960-80, failed to give plausible results for any of the four major Egyptian crops, wheat, rice, maize, and cotton, which indicates that Cuddihy's elasticity estimates are not valid for both periods.[42]

This result is not surprising nor does it prove that yields do not respond to changes in prices. During the period 1950-75, particularly in the second half of the period, developments affecting yields brought about major changes. The construction of the Aswan High Dam, which permitted secure perennial irrigation, allowed rice and maize area to expand into reclaimed desert land where the yield potential is lower. Water management problems and the rising water table reduced yields in some areas. Losses of fertile "old lands" to settlement offset reclamation of new lands, leading to a reduction in average yields. At the same time, increasing supplies of fertilizer and pesticide helped to balance some of these effects. Finally, changes in the availability of inputs and resources, such as labor and fertilizer, changed cropping patterns and intensities.

In sum, there is no simple way to assess acreage and yield response to price changes in Egypt in the short or medium run. The agricultural data available do not permit a satisfactory econometric analysis incorporating all the factors mentioned above. Moreover, constraints on resources, such as land and irrigation water, and shifts in the quality of resources, such as soils, cannot easily be taken into account. In principle, this problem could have been solved with a simultaneously estimated system.[43] But, because changes in prices in the past were modest, the parameter estimates would have been overstrained if used to analyze fundamental price policy changes, as is intended here. The effects a major change in the pricing system would have on allocation can hardly be derived from an econometric model that relies for information about the actual system on past data alone.

---

[41] See Cuddihy, *Agricultural Price Management in Egypt;* Bent Hansen and Karim Nashashibi, *Foreign Trade Regimes and Economic Development: Egypt* (New York: National Bureau of Economic Research, 1975); Hadi Esfahani and Alexander H. Sarris, "Agricultural Supply Response for the Main Crops in Egypt," Economics Working Paper 35, Agricultural Development Systems Project, Ministry of Agriculture, Cairo, and the University of California-Berkeley, Cairo, August 1981; and Joachim von Braun, "Agricultural Sector Analysis and Food Supply in Egypt," Interim Report of the Joint Project of the Institute of Agricultural Economics, University of Göttingen, and the Institute of National Planning, Cairo, February 1980 (mimeographed).

[42] Cuddihy, *Agricultural Price Management in Egypt,* pp. 32-41.

[43] Hansen and Nashashibi chose such an approach in their analysis for the 1960s. See Hansen and Nashashibi, *Foreign Trade Regimes and Economic Development: Egypt.*

Thus a programming model for agriculture is used to derive supply elasticities for specific products. Despite the well-known shortcomings of such models, they allow the relevant constraints to be incorporated more explicitly and policy instruments to be handled more flexibly. The responses of yield and area to prices are in fact artificial conceptualizations of production decisions that are actually made simultaneously. In that sense a programming model is closer to reality. The model analysis not only provides the required supply-response parameters for further analysis, but it gives additional information on the complex linkages within the sector.

Features of a Sector Model

The objective function of the model is to allocate resources in order to maximize farm income.[44] All prices are calculated at the farm gate. Resources are allocated according to the comparative advantages of alternative production activities at prices actually perceived by the producers. Price averages for the year 1979/80 are used. Demand is fixed for that year; hence trade is a residual, determined by domestic production and consumption. This seems to be a realistic specification given the government planning procedure for trade, which starts by defining food needs and calculates import demand and export supply considering supply from domestic sources.[45] This method of trade planning may also explain the low responsiveness of food imports to international price fluctuations.[46]

The model is of a static linear programming type. It incorporates 18 field crops and 5 animal products. Activities for each product usually consist of production, marketing, and either importation or exportation. For major field crops, fertilizer-yield functions are approximated. Other major activities are the provision of inputs, including draft animals, tractors, fertilizers, water, and labor. Water is endogenously distributed throughout the year, according to the monthly requirements resulting from the particular cropping pattern and constrained by the annual supplies from the High Dam. Labor is separated into a fixed family labor supply and a variable supply of hired labor.

The restrictions of the model include resource capacities differentiated by seasons or months, balances for variable factors such as feed and fertilizers, and crop rotation stipulations. Subsistence demand, which is fixed, is defined as consumption on a farm of its own produce. Trade restrictions account for constraints on the capacity of marketing institutions to successfully manage the quantities of products required. For example, the export traders that handle fruits and vegetables must be able to store them properly and to ship them promptly to avoid rotting. A constraint equal to their processing capacities is also placed on sugar processing. The government's intervention in area allocation and the enforced quotas are incorporated where applicable. The model includes 182 rows of 137 activities in its basic version. An extensive presentation of the entire model will not be furnished in this report.[47]

Production Structures under Different Price Regimes

The model analyzes the production effects of the different price regimes. It is a comparative static analysis. Changes in Egypt's agriculture that might result from changes in export marketing and from genetic and technical innovations are not explored. Insofar as price policy induces such changes, sectoral growth effects may be underestimated.[48]

The different price regimes are presented

---

[44] The structure of the model is presented in von Braun and de Haen, "Egypt and the EEC," p. 52.

[45] See Alderman, von Braun, and Sakr, *Egypt's Food Subsidy and Rationing System,* pp. 36-41.

[46] Scobie, *Government Policy and Food Imports.*

[47] The model is an updated and modified version of a model developed in a joint project of the Institute of Agricultural Economics, University of Göttingen and the Institute of National Planning, Cairo. Shawky Imam, of the University of Zagazig, contributed significantly to an earlier version of the model. A documentation of the current model is available from the authors. See von Braun, "Agricultural Sector Analysis and Food Supply."

[48] See, for example, the agricultural export production data in von Braun and de Haen, "Egypt and the Enlargement of the EEC," p. 53.

30

in five scenarios. Scenario 1 represents production and allocation in the present system, taking into consideration area allotment, delivery regulations, current product prices, and input prices. By comparing the actual structure of production and factor allocation, this scenario helps to explain the discrepancies between the model and reality (see Table 8). The discrepancies that arise are not always negligible, but to constrain them would reduce the flexibility of the model.

Scenarios 2 and 3 give some insights into the partial production effects of depressed cereal prices. Wheat prices are increased to their border price equivalents in scenario 2; the same is done for rice in scenario 3. Everything else stays the same as in scenario 1. Scenarios 2 and 3 yield hypothetical supply elasticities for the two crops. The implicit price elasticity of supply for wheat calculated from scenarios 1 and 2 is 0.26, and the one for rice, calculated from scenarios 1 and 3, is 0.59. This lies within the range of elasticities estimated econometrically by others for locations with similar agrarian structures and perennial irrigation.[49]

Under the rigid area allotment assumption for cotton, no cross effects may appear, but price increases for rice and wheat reduce maize and berseem production. This is the result of increased cropping intensity and of changes in area allocation.

A result of scenario 3 that is not immediately obvious is the increase in wheat production that follows an increase in rice prices (see Table 8). Rice production would increase mainly at the expense of maize, the other summer grain. Maize provides fodder in the fall. It is possible that only some of the roughage needed would be provided by imported maize concentrates. Therefore, wheat straw would be used as a supplemental fodder. The shadow prices of feed rise as a result (see the starch figures in Table 9). Wheat area is expanded, but the intensity of input use on wheat is reduced, because the by-product, wheat straw, which is now of major importance, is not as responsive to fertilizer as the wheat grain itself. The role wheat straw plays in the decision to grow wheat is stressed by this scenario where fodder is less available as a result of the decrease in maize.

Table 8—Effects of alternative agricultural pricing policies and government interventions on production, 1979/80

Commodity	Unit	Actual 1979/80	Scenario				
			1 Current System	2 Increased Wheat Price[a]	3 Increased Rice Price[a]	4 No Quotas or Area Restrictions	5 International Prices for All Inputs and Outputs
Wheat	1,000 metric tons	1,826	1,560	2,019	2,016	1,775	889
Beans and lentils	1,000 metric tons	237	283	283	283	228	393
Maize and sorghum	1,000 metric tons	3,628	3,093	3,093	2,267	3,245	2,374
Rice (paddy)	1,000 metric tons	2,448	2,299	2,531	3,796	2,298	3,318
Cotton (lint)	1,000 metric tons	498	485	485	485	485	536
Beef	1,000 metric tons	337	272	278	284	269	246

Sources: The actual figures for 1979/80 are from the Egyptian Ministry of Agriculture. The remaining figures are the results of computations made using the linear programming model of agriculture.

[a] This price is increased to the international equivalent.

[49] See Hossein Askari and John T. Cummings, *Agricultural Supply Response, A Survey of the Econometric Evidence* (New York: Praeger Publishers, 1976).

In scenario 3, the expansion of rice area leads to water scarcity. Water gets a shadow price, which it does not in scenario 1 (see Table 9). This too favors wheat production, as wheat requires about 30 percent less water than berseem, its major seasonal competitor.

Scenario 4 demonstrates the implications of direct government intervention in area allotment and marketing of food commodities. It is assumed that the area allotment for all crops but cotton is no longer enforced and no quota is required. Former quota prices are raised to equal domestic open market prices. This leads to increases in the production of wheat and maize and decreases in the production of pulses (beans and lentils). Rice area, formerly enforced by area allotment, declines, but increases in intensity. Its production is almost unaffected. Most of the abandoned rice area is taken over by maize.

Finally, scenario 5 uses international prices for all inputs and outputs. None of the crops are procured or their area restricted by the government. Under these conditions, production of maize, wheat, and beef drops considerably. When the livestock market is no longer protected, production of the fodder crops, wheat and maize, also declines.

On the other hand, cotton and rice production increase greatly. Feed requirements are balanced with increased berseem production and maize imports. Under the circumstances, the supply of draft power from the domestic buffalo and cattle herd becomes more scarce, which is indicated by an increased shadow price for horsepower and decreased shadow price for feed (Table 9). Gains from mechanization would be much higher under such conditions than under current conditions. Moreover, the shadow prices for land would decrease because the area sown with highly profitable crops would no longer be constrained by area allotments for low-price commodities. The water shadow price implies that under an international price regime and without area allocation, a water-pricing system would have to be introduced. This implication cannot be investigated in this study, but it indicates the need to tackle water management problems under a more market-oriented system.[50]

The water issue and the complex interactions of crop and livestock production illuminate the need for consistent sector modeling. The modeling exercise stresses that when agriculture is constrained by tight land resources, the frequently stated assumption that supply elasticities are greater

Table 9—Effects of alternative agricultural pricing policies and government interventions on shadow prices, 1979/80

		Scenario				
Shadow Prices	Unit	1 Current System	2 Increased Wheat Price[a]	3 Increased Rice Price[a]	4 No Quotas or Area Restrictions	5 International Prices for All Inputs and Outputs
Land, winter season	LE/feddan	176	179	143	176	115
Land, summer season	LE/feddan	110	112	55	110	69
Water	LE/1,000 cubic meters	. . .	. . .	18	. . .	8
Starch	LE/metric ton	144	146	165	144	142
Horsepower	LE/horsepower	·70	72	94	70	171

Sources: These are the results of computations made using the linear programming model of agriculture.

[a] This price is increased to the international equivalent.

---

[50] A more disaggregated modeling exercise that focuses particularly on the water issue is provided by Gary P. Kutcher, "The Agro-Economic Model," Master Plan for Water Resources Development and Use, Technical Report 16, Cairo, May 1980 (mimeographed).

than zero may not be realistic if all input and output prices vary simultaneously.[51] Reductions in supply are then possible, as cross-price effects might overcompensate own-price effects, even when prices as a whole rise. This is particularly relevant for Egypt where land is scarce and the water supply is inflexible.

One might argue that the total cultivated land base is also a function of agricultural prices. Land reclamation might increase if prices do. But this does not seem valid for a number of reasons. Land reclamation is mainly undertaken by the public sector and exogenously decided.[52] Neither the value of the crops to the economy at international prices nor the actual domestic prices appear to have affected the government's decision to expand crop land. Moreover, the new lands are exempt from any area allotment plan. Farmers are free to choose their optimal cropping pattern. Hence, changes in prices and price ratios for the basic food crops and cotton would not greatly affect returns from new lands, which are mostly devoted to fruits, vegetables, and fodder crops.

Addressing the other major concern of Egypt's agricultural policy, the decreasing self-sufficiency in major staples, the effect of a shift to international prices would be neutral. The decreases in the production of wheat and maize following such a change in price policy would be roughly offset by increased production of rice and pulses.

Whether so rigorous a change as a shift to world market prices would be socially optimal depends upon how risk aversive Egypt is.[53] An estimate of national risk aversion could be used to refine the assumption that international prices represent the opportunity costs of production. But no such estimate seems possible.

---

[51] Lutz and Scandizzo, for example, use supply elasticities assumed to range from 0.0 to 0.65 for a welfare analysis of Egypt's agricultural price policy on rice, cotton, and wheat. The higher elasticities lead to inconsistent results for production effects of the price distortions, assuming that elasticities being 0 is not plausible, given the indications of strong response to economic incentives from regression models. See Ernst Lutz and Pasquale L. Scandizzo, "Price Distortions in Developing Countries: A Bias against Agriculture," *European Review of Agricultural Economics* 7 (No. 1, 1980): 5-27.

[52] Gotsch and Dyer, "Rhetoric and Reason in the Egyptian 'New Lands' Debate," pp. 129-133.

[53] Sarris indicates that crops that are socially profitable when risk aversion is low (as it is for cash crops in Egypt) become less attractive when risk aversion is high and give way to subsistence crops. This reasoning, while valid, is not taken into account here. See Alexander H. Sarris, "Food Security and Agricultural Production Strategies Under Risk in Egypt," Working Paper 249, Division of Agricultural Sciences, University of California, Berkeley, March 1983 (mimeographed).

5

HOW FOOD SUBSIDIES AFFECT PUBLIC SPENDING ON AGRICULTURE

Since 1973 food subsidies, which were negligible in the 1960s, have accounted for 7 to 15 percent of total public expenditures. The additional drain on the budget in the 1970s had repercussions on other expenditures as they were not entirely financed by increased revenues or deficit spending. In analyzing the budget reallocation effects of food subsidies, the government's fiscal policy toward agriculture will be examined.

Problems in Analyzing Government Behavior

Unfortunately, most theories on how governments allocate funds are largely unrelated to each other; they seem to have only limited applicability to analyses of government behavior in systems with less formalized democratic structures and in developing economies.[54]

Attempts to study systematic patterns of government behavior for Egypt are aggravated by its recent history. The situation in the Middle East, the wars during the 1960s and early 1970s, the basic change in political-economic strategy in the 1970s, and the frequent reshuffling of institutions, such as the parliament (Peoples' Assembly), ministries, and political parties, are indications of that.

Because of these problems, this analysis is restricted to a descriptive approach. It may be looked at as an attempt to better understand the government's fiscal policy behavior. Some of the hypotheses underlying earlier models will be taken into consideration. But it is clear that any attempt to estimate these hypotheses empirically will encounter many difficulties.

Shifts in Patterns of Public Expenditures

Before an explanatory model of public spending on agriculture can be devised, basic changes in the size and structure of public spending must be examined. The actual decisionmaking process, its administrative setup, and political-economic determinants will be addressed later.

The following budget equation, which distinguishes between nonagricultural, agricultural, and food subsidy spending, holds for a given year (t):

$$R_t + D_t = N_t + A_t + F_t, \qquad (1)$$

where

R = government revenues,

D = the budget deficit,

N = nonagricultural expenditures (excluding food subsidies),

A = public expenditures for agriculture,

F = food subsidies, and

t = the index for the fiscal year.

The additional financial resources spent on food subsidies must be subtracted from means spent for nonagricultural or agricultural purposes, financed out of increased revenues, or financed through deficit spending. Thus:

$$\Delta F_{t,\,t-1} = \Delta R_{t,\,t-1} + \Delta D_{t,\,t-1} - \Delta N_{t,\,t-1} - \Delta A_{t,\,t-1}. \qquad (2)$$

---

[54] For a review of models tried, see Anthony B. Atkinson and Joseph E. Stiglitz, *Lectures on Public Economics* (New York: McGraw-Hill Book Co., 1980), pp. 294-330.

To begin with, some indications of government's behavior in the frame defined by equation (2) may be derived from a graphic analysis. Figures 4 and 5 show the dramatic changes in the size and structure of public expenditures that have occurred since 1972. These changes complicate any analysis of the effects of rising food subsidy bills, as other budget components also fluctuated considerably. During the period 1973-80, at the same time that food subsidies rose, there was rapid growth (in real terms) of all major budget components. Revenues rose mainly as a result of increased oil exports. Public-sector investments did not keep pace with these growth rates. The government's current expenditures increased dramatically as a result of a growing public-sector work force. In part, this expansion of the work force could be considered as an employment program. Military expenditures and losses in public-sector industries were also costly. The overall deficit increased sharply to more than 50 percent of the total budget in 1975, but has shrunk steadily since then.

The agricultural budget, which had been steadily declining since the mid-1960s, has grown in real terms since 1974 (see Figures 6 and 7). The rise in public expenditures in the mid-1970s reflects the end of the war burden and a reshuffling of the economy toward a more open and privately oriented system. GDP in real terms grew twice as fast during the period 1972-80 than during 1965-72 (7.3 percent versus 3.7 percent). The relationship between growth of GDP and public expenditure growth shows that Egypt is not an exception to Wagner's law of rising public expenditures in the growth process.[55] The expenditure elasticity of GDP rose to 1.8 during 1972-80, whereas it was unity for 1965-72 (see Table 10).

Agriculture was treated differently in the two time periods. Considering the importance to the economy of the employment and national income generated by agriculture, public investment in agriculture was low during the first period. Nevertheless, public investment contributed the major share of total investment in the sector. The negative expenditure elasticity of GDP (-0.79) for the sector during 1965-72 indicates that it was neglected. Investment in agriculture was cut back even more than total spending during this time. Although it rose remarkably in the 1970s, the shares of total public expenditure on agriculture and agricultural investment did not again become as large as they were in the mid-1960s (see Table 10). However, the growth of spending on agriculture was higher than the growth of total public expenditures.

Of course, negative expenditure elasticities for agriculture before subsidies became so prevalent (1965-72) and high positive ones during the time of extensive subsidy spending do not necessarily indicate a causal relationship between food subsidies and public expenditures on agriculture. Still, it is worth considering that gross fiscal support of agriculture was growing rapidly at the same time that agriculture's importance to the economy in the share of GDP and employment was shrinking (see Table 1). Thus, the idea that agriculture was suffering from absolute reductions in public spending when food subsidies were rising does not seem to be supported. A major reason for the support of agriculture may have been the dramatic decrease in self-sufficiency in basic food items during the 1970s, which was a matter of concern to those who formulate Egyptian food policy.

Changing Structures of the Agricultural Budget

Figures 6 and 7 show that the agricultural budget has undergone far-reaching structural changes. Input subsidies, mainly for fertilizer and pesticides, became a major component of the budget in the 1970s, whereas these commodities were slightly taxed in the 1960s. Other current expenditures were stable in real terms but their share decreased because expenditures on investment and input subsidies grew. In order to analyze

---

[55] Wagner's underlying hypothesis is that pressure for social considerations in the growth process is an additional driving force for increased public spending. This seems to be valid for Egypt as well. The extended social spending, among which food subsidies are a major element, is widely seen as a necessary social network in a period of rapid growth and structural change. See Richard A. Musgrave and Peggy B. Musgrave, *Public Finance in Theory and Practice* (Tokyo: McGraw-Hill Kogakusha, 1973), p. 116; and Alderman, von Braun, and Sakr, *Egypt's Food Subsidy and Rationing System,* pp. 13-18.

Figure 4—Deficits and revenues in public expenditure, 1965-80

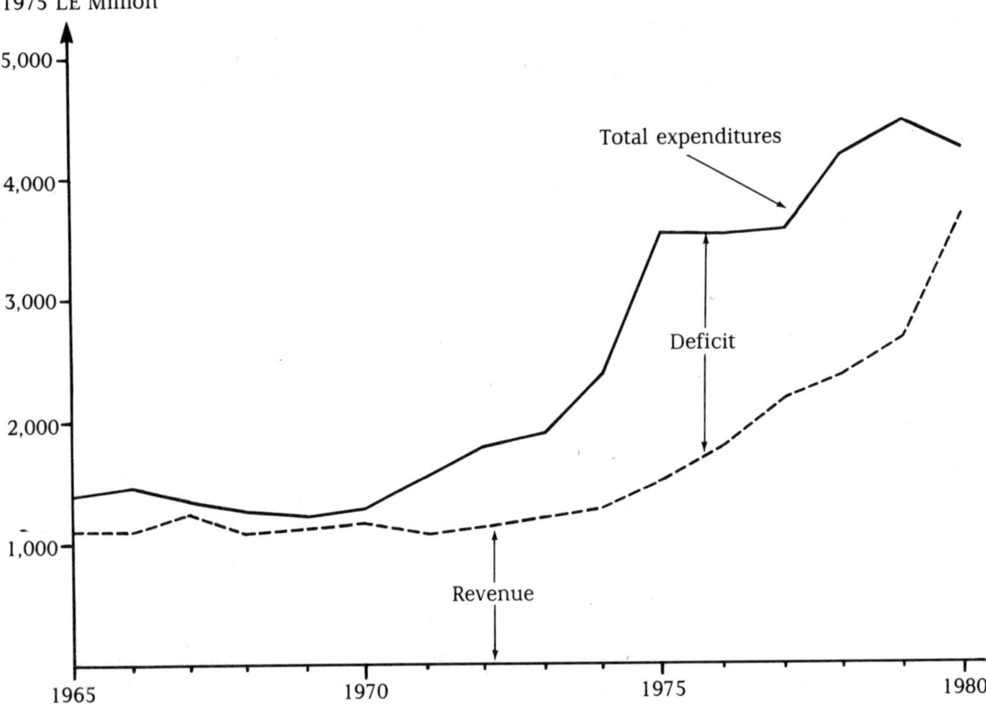

Sources: Calculations based on data from the Egyptian Ministries of Economy and Finance.

Figure 5—Structure of public expenditure, 1965-80

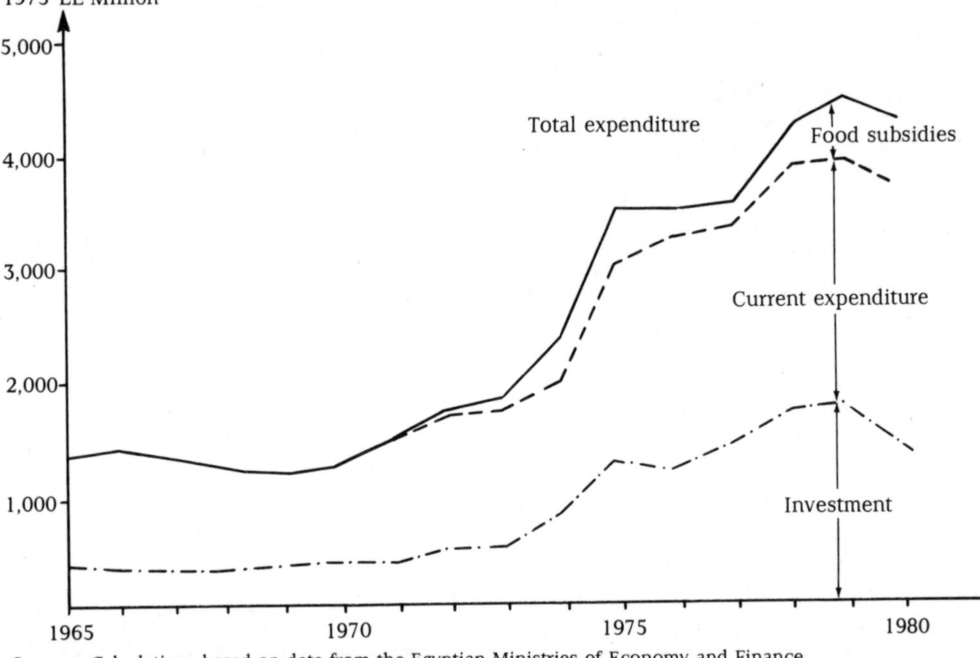

Sources: Calculations based on data from the Egyptian Ministries of Economy and Finance.

Figure 6—Government expenditures on agriculture, 1965-80

1975 LE Million

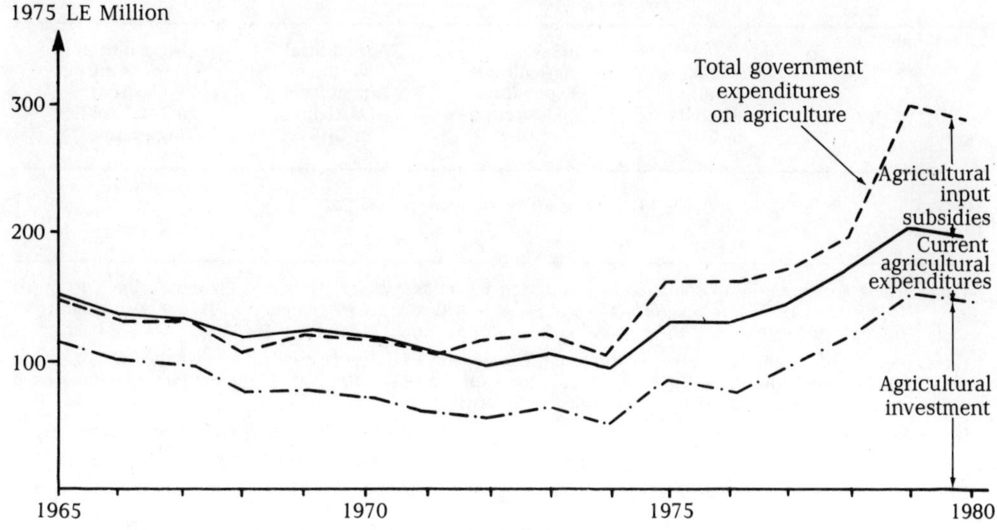

Sources: Calculations based on data from the Egyptian Ministries of Economy and Finance.

Figure 7—Share of agricultural investment, current expenditures, and input subsidies in total government expenditures, 1965-80

Percent of
Total Budget

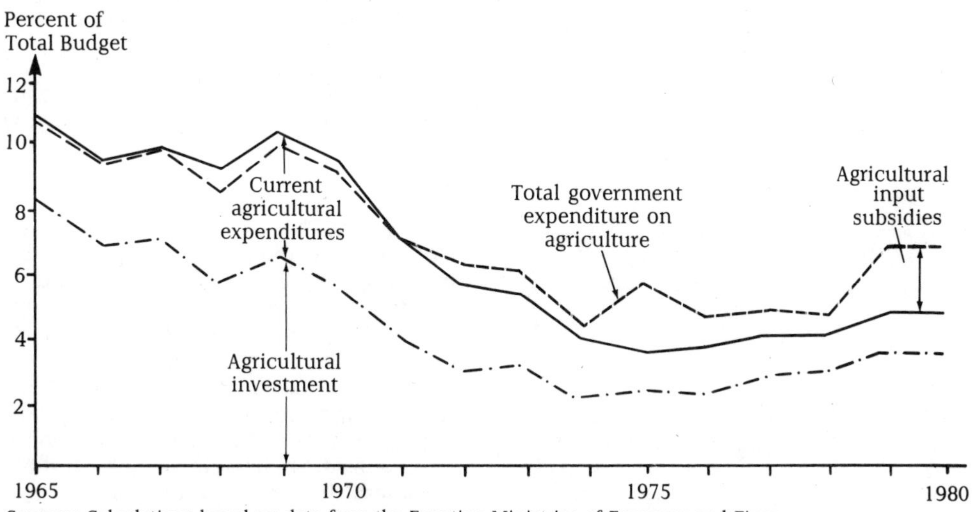

Sources: Calculations based on data from the Egyptian Ministries of Economy and Finance.
Note: Agricultural input subsidies showed small profits during 1965-71.

Table 10—Relationship between increases in public spending on agriculture, GDP, and total expenditures, 1965-72 and 1972-80

Period	Total Expenditure Elasticity of GDP[a]	Agricultural Expenditure Elasticity of GDP[b]	Agricultural Investment Expenditure Elasticity of GDP[c]	Agricultural Expenditure Elasticity of Total Public Expenditure[d]
1965-72	1.01	−0.79	−1.77	−0.78
1972-80	1.82	1.97	2.15	1.08

Sources: These are the results of computations using data from the Egyptian Ministry of Planning. The GDP figures from before 1977 were taken from World Bank statistics; the GDP figures for 1977-80 were taken from unpublished statistics of the Egyptian Ministry of Economy obtained in 1982.

[a] This is the ratio of the percentage increase in public expenditure to the percentage increase in the GDP. Note that the expenditure elasticities of the GNP are slightly lower for the 1972-80 period, as the net factor incomes from workers' remittances caused GNP to increase faster than GDP.

[b] This is the ratio of the percentage increase in public expenditures on agriculture to the percentage increase in GDP.

[c] This is the ratio of the percentage increase in agricultural investment expenditures to the percentage increase in GDP.

[d] This is the ratio of the percentage increase in public expenditures on agriculture to the percentage increase in total public expenditures.

these changes and their relation to spending on food subsidies within the budget framework, equation (1) is decomposed:

$$R_t + D_t = NC_t + NI_t + AC_t + AI_t + AS_t + F_t, \quad (3)$$

where

NC = nonagricultural current expenditures (excluding food subsidies),

NI = nonagricultural investment,

AC = agricultural current expenditures (excluding agricultural input subsidies),

AI = agricultural investment, and

AS = agricultural input subsidies.

The correlation coefficients of the shares of the components in total expenditures are shown in Table 11. It is widely assumed that food subsidies are positively correlated with the budget deficit; however, the correlation (0.51) turns out to be not very high. The negative correlation food subsidies have with public investment in agriculture, on the one hand, and the positive correlation they have with nonagricultural investment, on the other, are striking. This seems to contradict the general impression derived from the expenditure elasticities and the earlier graphic analysis. But the discrete comparison of two time periods does not take into account dynamic adjustments in the budget reallocation process. In fact, the share of food subsidies was at its height in 1974, when agricultural investment was lowest, both in real terms and as measured against total public expenditures. Though it shrank rapidly in the second half of the 1960s and the early 1970s in absolute terms, agricultural investment commanded a much higher share of the total budget than when food subsidies were rising. This explains the fairly high negative correlation (−0.74) estimated for the entire 1965-80 period. Nonagricultural investment, however, continued to grow, but at the cost of other budget components and a growing deficit.

While the traditional components of the agricultural budget—investment and current expenditures—decreased, the new one—input subsidies—increased, as did food subsidies. Thus there appears to be a high positive correlation between the two subsidies. Clearly, when import prices rose and uncontrolled domestic prices were inflated, the government attempted to stabilize both consumer prices and input prices. But, although correlation analysis provides information on the statistical relations between variables, one must refrain from interpreting coefficients in causal relationships.

Table 11 — Correlation coefficients of shares of budget components with special focus on the agricultural budget, 1965-80

Budget Component	Nonagricultural		Agricultural			Food Subsidies
	NC	NI	AC	AI	AS	F
D	−0.54	0.57	−0.75	−0.76	0.49	0.51
NC		−0.93	0.74	0.66	−0.72	−0.89
NI			−0.66	−0.69	0.59	0.71
AC				0.73	−0.84	−0.85
AI					−0.67	−0.74
AS						0.86

Notes: D stands for the budget deficit. NC is nonagricultural current expenditures, excluding food subsidies, and NI is nonagricultural investment. AC is current agricultural expenditures excluding agricultural input subsidies. AI stands for agricultural investment; AS, agricultural input subsidies; and F, food subsidies. Correlation coefficients for revenues are not listed as they are the same as for D, but with opposite signs.

The Role of Food Subsidies in Budgetary Decisionmaking

The national budget in Egypt is created by a complex procedure carried out by the established political institutions influenced by major political interest groups.[56] Technically, the budget is drafted by the Ministry of Finance in coordination with the ministries concerned. It is then discussed and modified in committees of the Peoples' Assembly and the Cabinet and delivered to the president, who presents it to the Peoples' Assembly for final approval.

The political decisionmaking on the national budget starts with an estimation of expected revenues and a limit set for the deficit. As subsidy allocations are given a high priority,[57] other budget components are adjusted to them. The actual food subsidy bill is determined mainly by fluctuations in international trade and the predetermined quantities to be channeled into the distribution system. Additional adjustments might be made if the international prices assumed differ from the real ones. Because revenues are fixed in the short run, short-term adjustments to subsidies are made in other current expenditures, deficits, and investments. Government-controlled consumer prices and rations are considered to be inflexible in this system, partly as a result of the consumer protests that occurred in the 1970s after attempts to alter consumer pricing.[58]

The agricultural budget currently involves three separate ministries: the Ministry of Agriculture and Food Security, the Ministry of Irrigation and the Sudan, and the Ministry of Reconstruction and Land Reclamation. Their investment budgets are handled mainly by state-owned companies, authorities for specific programs or crops, and regional agencies. Because the ministries themselves act only as consultants in setting agricultural price policy, their ability to generate revenues for agriculture is limited.[59]

The budget shares of preceding years are considered in decisionmaking by the cabinet. Consequently, the allocations for administration and investment of the three ministries handling agricultural affairs are fairly stable.[60] A large share of budget expenditures, such as administrative costs, is predetermined. The general size of the budget is a matter of political priority and changing it is not an issue in the short term.

---

[56] The authors are indebted to Ismail Badawy of the Ministry of Economy, Saad Barghout of the Ministry of Economy and the Ministry of Planning, and Yahya Mohie el-Din of the Ministry of Agriculture for clarification of this issue.

[57] See, for example, *Egyptian Gazette,* June 14, 1980, pp. 1-2.

[58] See Alderman, von Braun, and Sakr, *Egypt's Food Subsidy and Rationing System,* pp. 59-61.

[59] See Habashy, Fitch, and Rehiwi, "Egypt's Agricultural Cropping Pattern."

[60] The permanent budget hypothesis is discussed in O. A. Davis, M. A. H. Dempster, and A. Wildavsky, "A Theory of the Budgetary Process," *American Political Science Review* 60 (September 1966): 529-547.

The long-term reduction of agricultural investment in the 1960s and 1970s was apparently based on the assumption that marginal capital productivity would be smaller in agriculture than in other sectors. Agriculture grew less than expected following the construction of the Aswan High Dam. Discouraging results from capital-intensive efforts in new land reclamation may have contributed to this, too. Moreover, contraction and expansion of the agricultural budget are mainly determined by investment, which suffered from a change in attitude toward investment in reclaiming new land. Land reclamation accounted for about 80 percent of the agricultural investment budget between 1965/66 and 1971/72, but it was reduced to 51 percent by 1979/80.[61] Improvement of old land already under cultivation—through drainage projects, for example—and investment in research and development on animal production and specific crops took over an important share of the budget (see Figure 8).

The government provides an employment guarantee for university graduates. This adds an item to the budget that, like food subsidies, is exogenous to it. Increased enrollment and population growth of those in the relevant age groups is causing the number of graduates to grow rapidly. This has increased the wage bill of the public sector. The 1980 budget provided for 148,400 new jobs in government, mostly for graduates.[62] These new jobs represent an increase of about 8 percent of total government employees. The government actually took steps to abrogate the employment guarantee in 1979 but the policy was reversed in 1980. Redundancy seems unavoidable at such growth rates. But social and political objectives similar to those for consumer subsidies keep this policy in action.

The deficit in the national budget is a matter of continuous concern to the Egyptian government.[63] The inflationary implications of this deficit counteract the government's attempts to keep consumer prices down. But efforts to reduce the deficit require adjustment somewhere in the budget, which could affect spending on agriculture.

These statements can be transformed into hypotheses that can be tested in a regression model. One such hypothesis is that the ministerial bureaucracies attempt to defend their shares of the total budget. Another is that adjustments in the budget structure, and thus in agriculture, are enforced by exogenously fluctuating and predetermined components, such as food subsidies and other current expenditures of high priority. And a third is that the growth of the budget deficit, measured as a share of the total budget, induces cutbacks on expenditures, perhaps in agriculture.

For a regression model, a structural equation is written with the hypothetical signs of parameters defined as

$$a_t = \alpha + \beta_1 a_{t-1} - \beta_2 f_{t,t-1} - \beta_3 c_{t,t-1} - \beta_4 d_{t,t-1} + \Sigma_t, \quad (4)$$

where

a_t = the share of the agricultural budget in the total budget in year $t = ([AC_t + AI_t]/[R_t + D_t]) \cdot 100$;

$f_{t,t-1}$ = the change of the share of food subsidies in the total budget from the previous year to year $t = (F_t/[R_t + D_t] - F_{t-1}/[R_{t-1} + D_{t-1}]) \cdot 100$;

$c_{t,t-1}$ = the change of the share of nonagricultural current expenditures in the total budget from the previous year to year t (that is, total current expenditures less all subsidies), defined as equivalent to $f_{t,t-1}$;

$d_{t,t-1}$ = the change of the share of the overall deficit in the total budget from the previous year to year t, defined as equivalent to $f_{t,t-1}$; and

Σ_t = error term.

---

[61] Direct investment for the High Dam, which is not considered primarily an agricultural project, is not included in the comparison. Figure 8 shows it for illustrative purposes. Its inclusion would indicate an even more rapid shift away from new land reclamation policy.

[62] International Labour Organisation/United Nations Development Programme, "Employment Opportunities and Equity in a Changing Economy, Egypt in the 1980s," draft report of the ILO/UNDP Employment Strategy Mission, 1980 (mimeographed).

[63] See, for example, Egypt, Economic Conference, Document on Statement of Minister of Economy, Cairo, February 13-15, 1982. (In Arabic.)

Figure 8—Public investment in agriculture, 1965-80

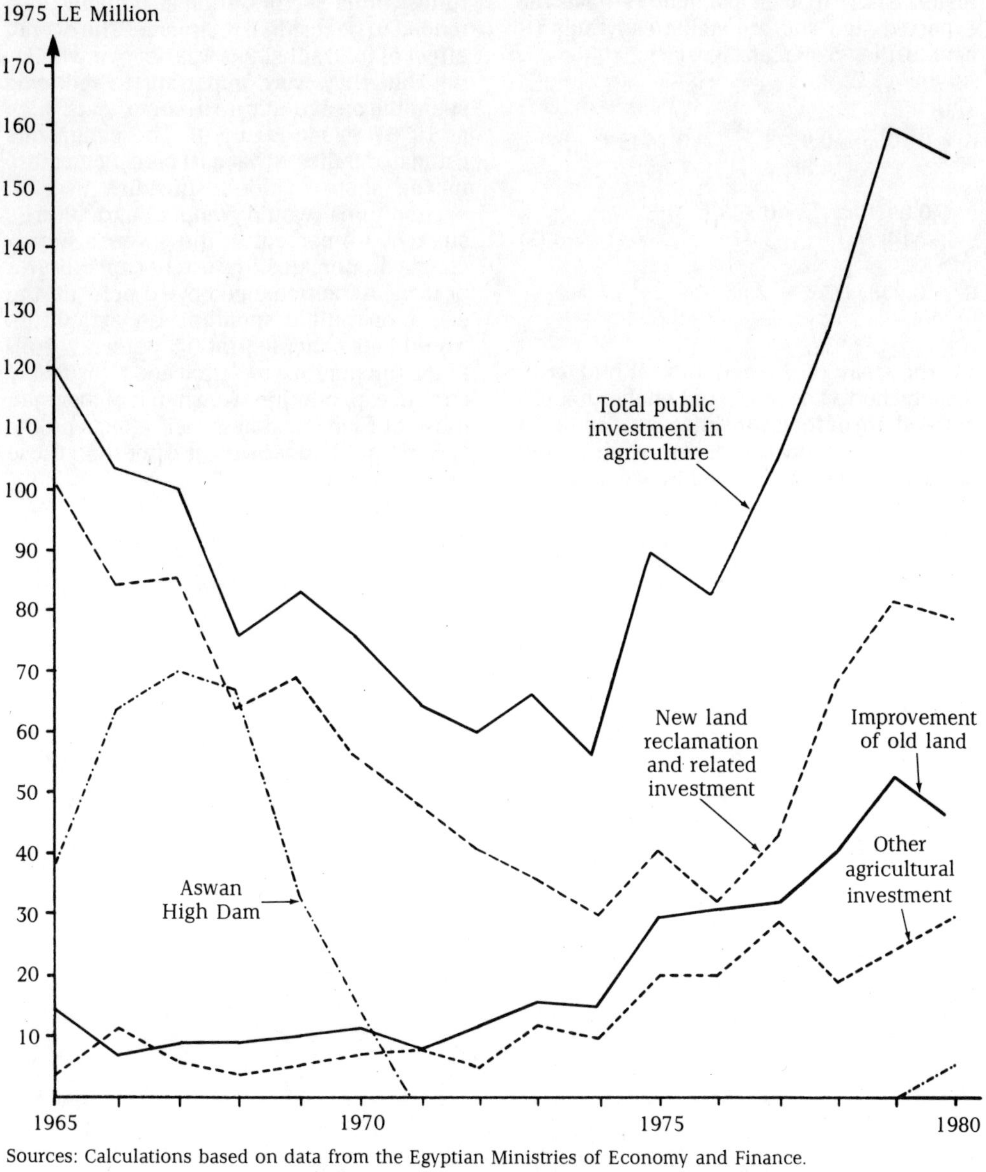

Sources: Calculations based on data from the Egyptian Ministries of Economy and Finance.

Notes: A tentative grouping of total public investment in agriculture is only possible because some of the titles cover several activities in different fields. Investment in the Aswan High Dam is not included in total public investment in agriculture.

41

The ordinary least square estimation results show that all parameters have the expected sign and are statistically significant at the 95 percent level:[64]

$$a_t = 0.1053 + 0.9523\ a_{t-1} - 0.1445\ f_{t,\,t-1}$$
$$(14.87)\phantom{a_{t-1} -}(-1.85)$$

$$- 0.0919\ c_{t,\,t-1} - 0.535\ d_{t,\,t-1};$$
$$(-2.14)\phantom{c_{t,t-1}}(-3.47)\phantom{d_{t,t-1};}\qquad(5)$$

$$\hat{R}^2 = 0.958,\ \text{D.W.} = 2.96.$$

The share of the agricultural budget in the total budget decreased when the changes of the share of food subsidies, other current expenditures, and the deficit were rising. Though its share in the total budget is small, agriculture was a residual recipient of public funds. Other sectors, such as housing, also tended to be residual recipients. The overall effect of food subsidies was not overwhelming, but they were important in reducing spending on agriculture in some years, such as 1973/74 (see Figure 9). The parameters estimated indicate that a 10 percent increase in the share of food subsidies in total expenditures would reduce agriculture's share by 1.4 percent. If there were a similar change in nonsubsidy current expenditures or if the deficit changed by 10 percent, the effect on public spending on agriculture would be smaller (0.9 or 0.5 percent). Still, as the fluctuations of deficit and nonsubsidy current expenditures were much higher than those of food subsidies, their effects on the agricultural budget were greater than those of food subsidies.

---

[64] The Durbin-Watson statistic indicates that the parameters estimated may not be free from distortions because of autocorrelation of residuals. But intercorrelations between $f_{t,\,t-1}$, $c_{t,\,t-1}$, and $d_{t,\,t-1}$, are so small (f:c=−0.56, f:d=0.18, c:d=−0.04) that they do not cause distortions from that side.

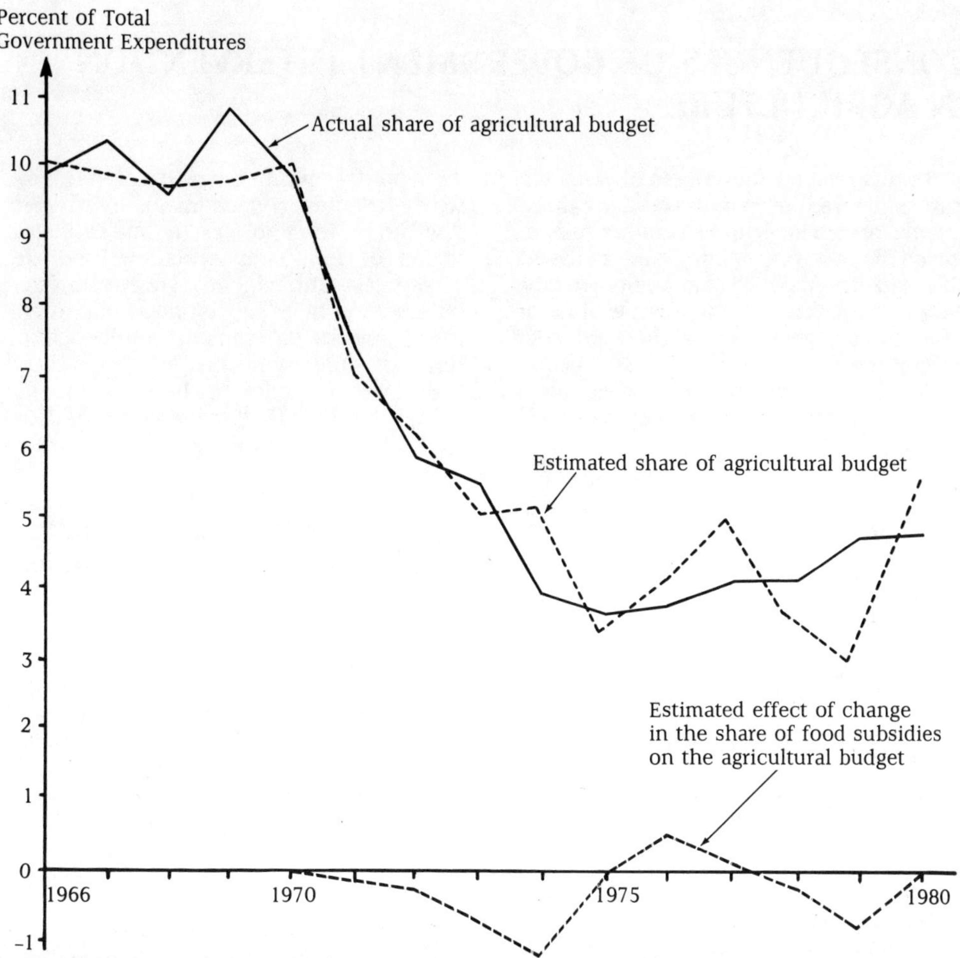

Sources: Calculations based on data from the Egyptian Ministries of Economy and Finance.
Notes: The change in the share of food subsidies in the agricultural budget was calculated from equation (4). It is
the estimated parameter β_2 multiplied by observed values of $f_{t,t-1}$.

6

CONSEQUENCES OF GOVERNMENT INTERVENTION IN AGRICULTURE

In this chapter the effects of price and market intervention policies on agricultural income, on producer and consumer welfare, and on the government budget are analyzed. This market analysis by commodity provides the groundwork for a final policy evaluation based on an assessment of the burden on agriculture.

All major agricultural commodities listed below are included in the market analysis:[65]

Commodity	Percent of Cropped Area 1979/80
Wheat and wheat products	12.5
Rice	9.3
Maize	16.8
Beans	2.6
Lentils	0.2
Sugar	2.2
Cotton	10.7
Beef	. . .
Milk and milk products	. . .
Feed	
Berseem	24.8
Sorghum, barley	4.8
Concentrates	. . .
Inputs	
Fertilizer	. . .
Pesticides	. . .

About 84 percent of the agricultural area is covered by these crops. The share of these major commodities in household expenditures on food is about 73 percent.[66]

A partial equilibrium model of the market for each of these commodities is constructed. The model incorporates the major instruments of food and agricultural policies affecting it, which include government procurement policies, government import and export policies, government food distribution schemes, dual pricing on both the producer and consumer sides of the market, input subsidies for the field crops, and subsidized feed distribution to livestock producers.

Theoretical Basis for Evaluating the Effects of Price Distortions

Gains and losses from price distortions are derived using a comparative static computation of economic surplus for major agricultural commodities. The procedure is well known and its merits and its shortcomings have been frequently discussed.[67] However, a few clarifications are necessary for this study.

To know what gains and losses are produced by the price distortions and government interventions induced by subsidies requires knowledge of the prices (and production technology) that would prevail in a hypothetical situation with or without reduced food subsidies. If food subsidies were the only reason for interventions in the agricultural markets, one would expect that without subsidies there would be free trade, with world market prices also serving as domestic prices to producers and consumers. But government interventions have other

---

[65] These percentages are calculated from unpublished data provided by the Ministry of Agriculture, Institute of Agricultural Economics, Research, and Statistics, Cairo, 1982.

[66] In 1974/75 household expenditures on wheat, rice, maize, beans, lentils, sugar, meat, and milk and milk products accounted for 76 percent of the average total expenditure on food in rural households and 68 percent in urban ones (Egypt, Central Agency for Public Mobilization and Statistics, *Family Budget Survey, 1974/75* [Cairo: CAPMAS, 1978]).

[67] See J. M. Currie, J. A. Murphy, and A. Schmitz, "The Concept of Economic Surplus and its Use in Economic Analysis," *Economic Journal* 81 (December 1971): 741-799; and J. Lesourne, *Cost-Benefit Analysis and Economic Theory* (Amsterdam and Oxford: Elsevier-North Holland, 1975).

purposes as well. For example, the prices of export crops are taxed in order to increase government income, and some livestock products are protected in order to stimulate domestic production. As long as policy goals other than keeping food prices low exist, one cannot assume that a removal of food subsidies would result in free trade prices. Prices would lie somewhere between current and world market prices. Without an explanatory model of agricultural policy decisions, it is impossible to separate observed price distortions according to the policy goals and instruments behind them.

Despite this, world market prices are used as a basis for computing the sum of all policy-induced distortions. There are several reasons why this seems acceptable. First, the assurance of low-cost food supplies, managed through import subsidies, is clearly the dominant goal of agricultural policies in Egypt. Imports, apart from food aid, distributed domestically at subsidized prices are paid for at international prices, and thus represent the opportunity cost. Second, even those interventions in agriculture that are motivated by taxation objectives may stem indirectly from food subsidies, insofar as subsidies are a prominent reason for the persistent budget deficit in Egypt. Moreover, distortions induced by policy provide a basis for an analysis in which the objectives of policy are formulated as exogenous determinants of the development of the distortions (see Chapter 7).

Price distortions in the following analysis are defined as the divergence between the price of a good at the farm gate (producer price distortions) or at the Cairo retail market (consumer price distortions) and the corresponding international price. International prices are evaluated at the shadow exchange rate and adjusted for transportation costs and state of processing. The price wedge resulting from the comparison for producers is corrected further to include the input subsidies for each unit of output (see Chapter 3).

The computations of the effects of price distortions in major commodity markets on welfare and the budget during the period 1965-80 were made using the following equations. Where relevant, a distinction is made between controlled and free markets.[68]

The net social loss in production (NSL_p) is

$$NSL_p = \tfrac{1}{2}(Q_w - Q)(P_w - P_p^o) = \tfrac{1}{2} t_p^2 \eta_s V; \quad (5)$$

where

Q	= production at domestic prices,
Q_w	= production at world prices,
P_w	= border price equivalent at the shadow exchange rate,
P_p^o	= producer price on the uncontrolled open market,
t_p, t_c	= proportion of tariff in the domestic producer or consumer price on the open market ($[P_w - P_p]/P_p$ or $[P_w - P_c]/P_c$),
η_s, η_d	= supply and demand multipliers, measured as the relative change of quantities of a commodity in response to changes of its own price after a shift of all prices to free trade prices, and
V	= value of production at P_p^o.

The net social loss in consumption (NSL_c) is

$$NSL_c = \tfrac{1}{2}(C_w - C)(P_c^o - P_w) = \tfrac{1}{2} t_c^2 \eta_d R; \quad (6)$$

where

P_c^o	= consumer price on the uncontrolled open market,
C	= consumption at domestic prices,
C_w	= consumption at world prices, and
R	= value of consumption at P_c^o.

The welfare gain of producers (G_p) is

$$G_p = Q^f(P_p^f + s - P_w) +$$
$$(Q - Q^f)(P_p^o + s - P_w) - NSL_p; \quad (7)$$

---

[68] The nomenclature and structure closely follow Bale and Lutz. See Malcolm D. Bale and Ernst Lutz, "Price Distortions in Agriculture and their Effects: An International Comparison," *American Journal of Agricultural Economics* 63 (January 1981): 8-22.

where

P_p^f = fixed procurement price,

Q^f = procurement of domestic supplies, and

s = direct input subsidy per unit of output.

The welfare gain of consumers (G_c) is

$$G_c = C^f (P_w - P_c^f) + (C - C^f)(P_w - P_c^o) - NSL_c; \quad (8)$$

where

P_c^f = fixed consumer price, and

C^f = consumption out of government supplies at fixed prices.

An increase in budget expenditures (TB) is

$$TB = Q_d^f (P_p^f + s + k_d - P_c^f)$$
$$+ (Q^f - Q_d^f)(P_p^f + s + k_d - P_w^r)$$
$$+ M(P_w^r + k_m - P_g^m); \quad (9)$$

where

k_d, k_m = costs of processing, marketing, and transporting of either procured quantities or imports,

Q_d^f = procured quantity sold to domestic consumers (the rest is exported),

P_w^r = border price equivalent at the official exchange rate,

P_g^m = release price of the imported commodity going either to consumers or to feed users, and

M = imports.

The computation of the net social losses of supply and demand is complicated by the hypothetical amounts produced and consumed at world prices, which are supposed to result not only from a change of their own prices but from adjustments of all other prices as well. Hence, to assure consistent analysis, the parameters η_s and η_d in equations (5) and (6) are not defined as the usual price elasticities of supply and demand, which hold true only if nothing but the own price of a respective commodity changes, but as implicit multipliers of quantities relative to a change in the own price accompanying changes in other prices (P_j, with $j = 1, \ldots, m$), which set them equal to world market prices.

Let Q_i be a linear supply function of commodity i, with β representing the parameters.[69] Thus,

$$Q_i = \beta_{io} + \sum_{j=1}^{m} \beta_{ij} \, P_j. \quad (10)$$

The relative change of production, Q_i, resulting from changes in all prices, can then be written:

$$\Delta Q_i = \sum_{j=1}^{m} \beta_{ij} \, \Delta P_j. \quad (11)$$

Inserting this into equation (5) gives the net social loss in production:

$$NSL_{pi} = \tfrac{1}{2} \sum_{j=i}^{m} \beta_{ij} \, \Delta P_j \cdot \Delta P_i, \quad (12)$$

where $\Delta P_i = P_{wi} - P_{pi}^o$.

Defining the multiplier, η_s, as the relative change of production per unit of a relative change of the own price, measured as a response to a simultaneous change of all prices, one obtains:[70]

$$\eta_{si} = (\Delta Q_i / \Delta P_i)(P_i / Q_i)$$
$$= \sum_{j=1}^{m} \beta_{ij} \Delta P_j [(1/\Delta P_i)(P_{pi}^o / Q_i)]. \quad (13)$$

Inserting equation (13) into (12) and rearranging the expression as indicated in the second term of equation (5) gives:

$$NSL_{pi} = \tfrac{1}{2} \eta_{si} \cdot \Delta P_i (Q_i / P_{pi}^o) \Delta P_i$$
$$- \tfrac{1}{2} \eta_{si} (\Delta P_i / P_{pi}^o)^2 Q_i P_{pi}^o , \text{ or}$$
$$= \tfrac{1}{2} \eta_{si} t_p^2 \cdot V. \quad (14)$$

---

[69] The procedure implies the usual assumption that the supply function is identical to the marginal cost function. Moreover, it is assumed that the changes in cross prices indicate changes in opportunity costs.

[70] The definition implies that marginal costs vary linearly between the two levels of production computed in the model scenario.

Figure 10 shows the theoretical approach to measuring the welfare loss of producers when deliveries at fixed prices are forced, the open market is residual, and price distortions exist for competing production enterprises.[71]

Producers are forced to deliver a quantity, Q^f, of a certain agricultural commodity at a fixed price, P_p^f. An additional quantity, $Q - Q^f$, is supplied on the open market at an open market price, P_p^o. Both the fixed price and the open market price are below the world market price. A partial switch of the producer price, P_p^o, to the world market price, with all other producer prices remaining unadjusted, would yield an elastic response from H to M. Yet if the prices of competing products are also raised, the supply curve is likely to be shifted to the left and a dampened production increase, say from H to L, may result.

Compared to this hypothetical free-trade situation, the producers currently suffer a welfare loss (producers' rent forgone in the production of commodity i) of DEGHLI. This welfare loss is composed of a loss through forced deliveries, DEJI; a loss through distortions on open markets, GHKJ; and a calculated loss through reduced production and misallocation, HLK (which equals NSL_p).

Elasticities for these computations were calculated in a partial equilibrium framework from the relative differences in production between scenario 5 of the programming model (world prices, no government interventions) and scenario 1 (distorted prices, area allotment, procurement, and input subsidies) using the relative difference between world market and domestic open market prices as a denominator.

These model results provide implicit elasticities of the response of production to a simultaneous change of prices to their international equivalents (η_s):[72]

Commodities	Implicit Supply Elasticities
Wheat	-0.38
Rice	0.28
Maize (and sorghum)	-0.67
Beans	1.46
Lentils	0.33
Sugar	0.01
Cotton	0.07
Beef and milk	0.19
Nitrogen fertilizer	-0.03

A coefficient of 0.1 is used for sugar in the consecutive analysis as an assumption for possible yield effects that are not incorporated in the model for that crop. The elasticities for beef and milk are a weighted average, the weights being the shares in value of production.

These elasticities are strictly valid only for 1979/80, the base year of the linear programming solution. The difference between production in the two scenarios is typical of a long-run solution during the period of analysis, 1965-80. Therefore the elasticities of supply for any year within this period are derived by dividing the relative deviation of the quantities computed by the linear programming model by the nominal rate of taxation during the respective year.

The demand parameters for the analysis are obtained from a complete demand system. The model was estimated as a linear expenditure system based on a time series of cross-sections of household expenditure surveys for 1958/59, 1964/65, and 1974/75.[73] It distinguishes between three levels of household expenditure within the rural and urban population. The own-price elasticities for the weighted average of several groups are listed in Appendix 2.[74]

The approach chosen here combines the results from a programming model of the

---

[71] For simplification, input subsidies are neglected in the graphic presentation.

[72] Note that these elasticities take into account simultaneous shifts in production and intermediate use of other commodities (see equation 13). They are not equivalent to the common definition of elasticities that hold true under the condition that all other prices remain unchanged.

[73] The data bases are taken from Egypt, Central Agency for Public Mobilization and Statistics, *Family Budget Survey 1958/59* (Cairo: CAPMAS, 1961); CAPMAS, *Family Budget Survey 1964/65* (Cairo: CAPMAS, 1972); and CAPMAS, *Family Budget Survey 1974/75.*

[74] The system is described in detail in Joachim von Braun, "A Demand System for Egypt—Estimation Results and Scenario Analysis for Alternative Food Price Policies," Institute of Agricultural Economics, University of Göttingen, December 1981 (mimeographed).

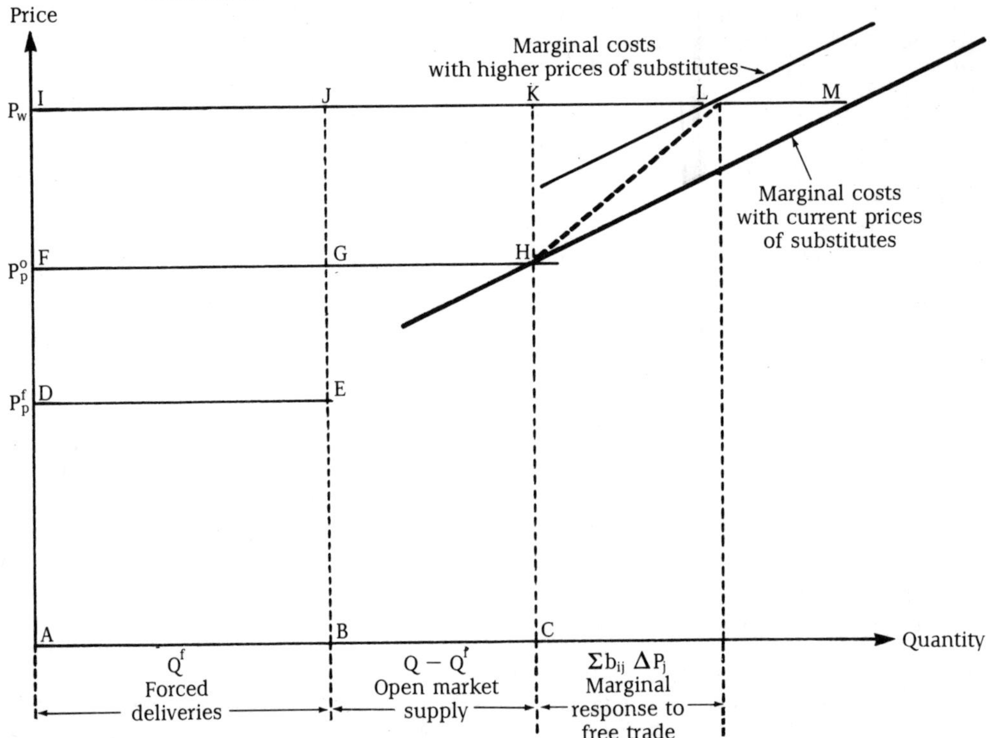

Figure 10—Welfare losses of producers resulting from price distortions and procurement

sector with partial equilibrium models for individual commodities. It is an attempt to avoid inconsistencies of partial equilibrium analyses, on the one hand, and the methodological and statistical problems of dynamic multicommodity sector models, on the other. This approach does not eliminate these problems completely, as dynamic adjustments are not endogenously taken care of, but it provides for a more realistic and practical solution than either of the two approaches used alone.

Grain Markets

The three major cereals produced in Egypt—wheat, rice, and maize—are affected in different ways by agricultural policy and their market structures do not have much in common. The producer prices of all three, especially wheat and rice, are kept below international prices. As stated earlier, the government procures rice and wheat but not maize. Although procurement for rice is compulsory, with a per feddan quota, a similar regulation for wheat was almost phased out in 1977 (see Chapter 3). Imports of wheat and maize are distributed at subsidized prices but the former is channeled to consumers while the latter goes mainly to livestock producers.

The Wheat Market

In the late 1970s Egypt's domestic wheat production covered about 25 percent of total consumption. Procurement of the domestic crop dropped from an average of 20 percent of production in 1974-75 to 10 percent in 1978-80 after the enforcement of procurement was relaxed.

Domestic prices are depressed below their international equivalents, which places a burden on wheat producers. This burden may be split into three different sources: procurement (G_{prc}^p); depression of the free market price (G_{fre}^p); and inefficiency in the allocation of resources for production, which is usually referred to as net social loss in production (G^p_{soc}) (see Figure 11). Note that the social loss in production may in fact be negative in some years. If all prices are raised toward international prices, the supply curve of wheat would shift to the left, as the sector model results indicate.

Consumers gain from the subsidy on wheat flour and bread (G^c_{dis}). But they also gain from the reduction in open market prices net of the misallocation to consumption ($G^c_{fre} - G^c_{soc}$). Most of these gains, which increase demand, are covered by government subsidies on wheat imports or procured domestic wheat, and part is indirectly financed by the wheat producers (G^p_{prc}, G^c_{fre}).

Subsidized fixed consumer prices ranged from 28 to 58 percent of the international wheat price during the period 1965-80 (see Table 12), and were slightly higher than government procurement prices during the 1960s.[75] This means the government was able to generate revenues from domestic procurement policy, which was compulsory at that time. During the 1970s the procurement prices usually exceeded the average fixed consumer price. The uncontrolled price of wheat in rural markets fluctuated much more than the fixed procurement and consumer prices but always exceeded both of them. The gap between fixed and open market prices was particularly high in years of political crises, such as 1967, when the gap was 40 percent, and 1973, when the gap was 38 percent. Both years, a war coincided with a major exogenous shock to the country's wheat supply: in 1966/67 the United States, which had covered 35-50 percent of the country's wheat imports during the early 1960s, stopped giving food aid to Egypt for political reasons, and in 1973/74 the international food price crisis began. Open market prices also far exceeded fixed prices in 1978, for several reasons. Imports decreased in that year, possibly because foreign exchange was tight. And consumer prices of maize were unusually high because of a shortage of feed concentrates. This may

have contributed to the rise in wheat prices in rural areas, which worsened the food situation of the poor.[76]

Most open market wheat comes from domestic production. Some is subsidized wheat flour from government distribution channels that is resold. However, as the share of open market wheat in the total wheat supply is falling rapidly, fluctuations in the supply from the government distribution system will increase instability in this residual market. During 1969-71 the average supply of wheat from domestic production left after procurement accounted for 31 percent of total consumption. This dropped to 24 percent in the 1978-80 period. Moreover, only some of this entered the market because wheat is a major subsistence crop for the farm population.[77]

The international wheat price used in the analysis is the reported value of a unit of wheat corrected for handling costs and for the overvaluation of the Egyptian pound (see Appendix 1, Table 32). For the calculation of the producer losses and consumer gains, it should reflect the marginal import price. However, Egypt receives significant amounts of food aid and concessional imports. In 1980 they accounted for about 30 percent of all wheat imported. If the quantities and prices of commercial imports were functions of concessional imports and given that re-exports of wheat are restricted under the regulations for food aid disposal of the Food Aid Convention, the unit value would overstate the opportunity cost of producing wheat in Egypt.[78]

The marginal import price, which matters in assessing the opportunity costs of wheat products in Egypt, would only be affected by food aid donations if all commercial wheat exporters to Egypt were also food aid donors, providing aid through a tight relationship to commercial sales. A somewhat systematic pattern in the ratios between commercial imports and concessional im-

---

[75] The fixed consumer price is calculated here as a weighted average of subsidized bread and flour prices in wheat grain equivalents.

[76] See Alderman, von Braun, and Sakr, *Egypt's Food Subsidy and Rationing System,* p. 59.

[77] Estimations of marketed surplus based on data of household surveys yield a share of 21 percent of total consumption out of marketed domestic production for 1969-71 and 15 percent for 1978-80 respectively (CAPMAS, *Family Budget Survey, 1974/75*). Constant per capita wheat consumption from own production is assumed for the farm population in this calculation.

[78] The Food Aid Convention is part of the International Wheat Agreement of 1967, which was amended in 1981 (International Wheat Council, *International Wheat Agreement, 1981* [London: International Wheat Council, n.d.]).

Figure 11 — Average conditions in the wheat market, 1976-80

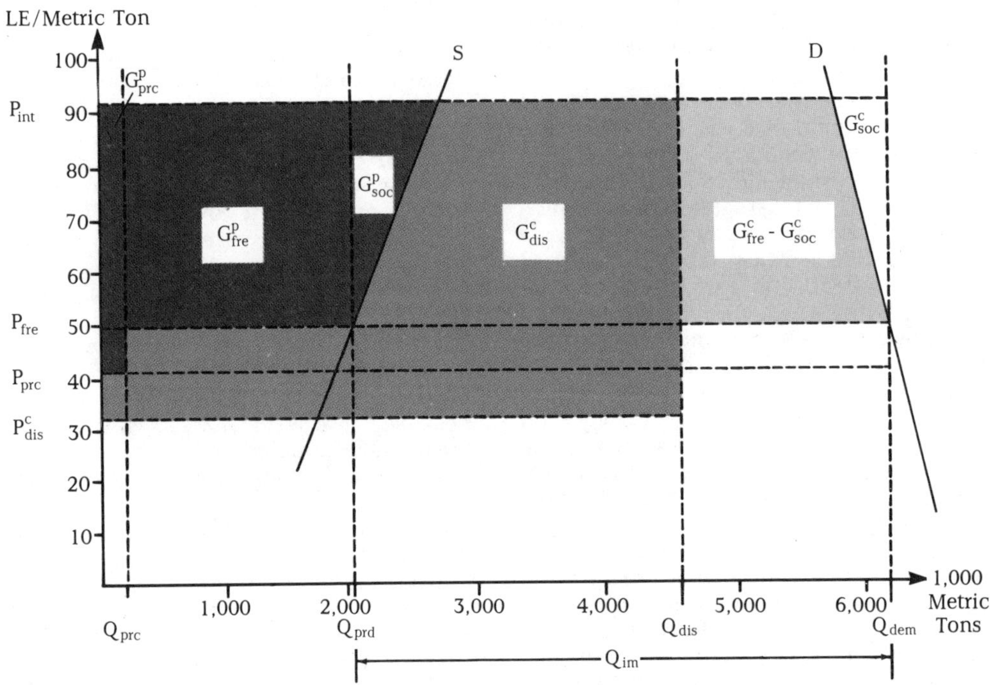

Sources: Calculated from data provided by the Egyptian Ministries of Agriculture and Supply and the Principal Bank for Development and Agricultural Investment.

Notes: Prices are deflated by the consumer price index (1975 = 100). P_{int} is the international price, P_{fre} is the open market price, P_{prc} is the government procurement price, and P^c_{dis} is the fixed consumer price. Q_{prd} is domestic production (total), Q_{prc} is government procurement of domestic production, Q_{dis} is government distribution ($Q_{prc} + Q_{im}$), Q_{dem} is total consumption, and Q_{im} is imports (= $Q_{dem} - Q_{prd}$). S is supply; D is demand.
G^p_{prc} is the producers' loss from government procurement, G^p_{fre} is the producers' loss from depression of the free market price, and G^p_{soc} is the net social loss in production. G^c_{dis} is the consumers' gain from the distribution of wheat flour and bread. (The consumers' gain also includes G^p_{fre}, G^p_{prc}, and G^p_{soc} in the figure.) G^c_{fre} is the consumers' gain from reduced free market prices, and G^c_{soc} is misallocation in consumption. For further details see Appendix 2.

ports from major donors indicates that such a condition may not be completely excluded for some time periods.[79]

Yet trade and aid statistics do not show that food aid is permanently tight. Food aid policies toward Egypt have changed as Egypt's political role in the Middle East has changed. The terms for aid from the U.S.S.R. in 1967/68 were different from those imposed by Australia, during the years when no U.S. food aid was available, and the terms for U.S. aid during the first half of the 1960s differed from those set during the second half of the 1970s.

In recent years Egypt has relied increasingly less on short-term open tenders and more on long-term bilateral import agreements to acquire wheat. The actual price of

---

[79] Food aid made available from other countries such as the European Community and Australia and Canada increased considerably when these countries became major grain exporters to Egypt following the political frictions between the United States and Egypt in 1966, which led to cancellation of U.S. food aid. After food aid flows from the United States were reestablished in 1973, the trade and aid by countries shifted closer to previous patterns. See Joachim von Braun, "Effects of Food Aid in Recipient Countries: Egypt and Bangladesh, a Comparative Study," in *Economics: A Biannual Collection of Recent German Contributions to the Field of Economic Science*, vol. 26 (Tübingen: Institut für Wissenschaftliche Zusammenarbeit, 1982), pp. 18-47.

Table 12—Relationship of wheat prices to international and open market prices, 1965-80

Year	Share of International Price			Share of Open Market Price	
	Procurement Price	Open Market Producer Price	Fixed Consumer Price	Procurement Price	Fixed Consumer Price
	(percent of border price)			(percent of open market price)	
1965	36.9	49.4	42.6	74.9	86.3
1966	43.4	61.5	43.7	70.6	71.1
1967	44.4	75.6	45.8	58.8	60.6
1968	50.4	92.0	58.1	54.8	63.1
1969	48.1	66.6	53.5	72.3	80.4
1970	50.1	65.2	48.3	76.8	74.0
1971	57.2	70.0	56.1	81.7	80.2
1972	58.3	69.1	56.7	84.3	82.1
1973	29.6	41.5	30.0	71.3	72.2
1974	29.0	38.5	29.6	75.2	76.8
1975	35.3	43.8	31.9	80.6	72.9
1976	39.4	45.7	36.7	86.2	80.4
1977	53.2	66.6	47.1	79.9	70.7
1978	49.8	77.2	44.4	64.4	57.5
1979	45.5	48.6	32.4	93.6	66.7
1980	41.5	45.7	28.4	90.7	62.2

Sources: These figures were computed from data provided in 1982 by the Egyptian Ministry of Agriculture, the Central Agency for Public Mobilization and Statistics, and the Ministry of Supply.

Note: The border price is calculated from values of imports, with marketing costs added and corrections made to account for the overvaluation of the currency (see Table 32).

wheat imports under long-term agreements is less than the contracted values. For example, the current agreement with France and the United States requires repayment at interest rates significantly below market rates. In fact, the import price for Egypt (P_{int}) is not a straight line, as drawn for simplification in Figure 11, but a step function. The lowest steps are represented by cost-free wheat donations, such as those from the World Food Programme (WFP) and some European Community and U.S. aid shipments. The next lowest steps would be the U.S. P.L. 480, Title I concessional imports, which have 40-60 percent of their cost subsidized if the long-term loans are discounted at prevailing market rates. Another step would be formed by imports acquired under easy repayment terms, such as those provided under agreements with Australia, France, or the United States, and the highest step would be composed of actual commercial imports at current international prices.

Using the unit values or marginal price of imports does not impede the calculation of the welfare loss of producers, but using unit values to compute the fiscal costs of wheat imports does require some explanation. Whereas the short-term fiscal outlay may be exaggerated by using unit values, which do not take into account long-term repayment schedules for imports acquired with soft loans, the long-term effects on the budget of soft-loan imports would be neglected if the actual installment payments for them were used in the calculation. Ideally, the actual installment payments for imports in the current year and all previous years should enter the calculation of the fiscal effects of wheat imports, but the data are not available in time series.

The following results were obtained from the market analysis. In 1980 wheat producers had an income loss of LE 134 million (G_{tot}^p in Appendix 2, Table 35). Although the income losses of producers fluctuated considerably during the 1960s and 1970s because international prices and domestic open market prices were unstable, they do not show a trend in any direction. Expressed in 1975 prices, they shrank from the peaks of 1974-78, but increased again in 1979 and 1980 (see Table 13). Losses from procurement have been minor in recent years. In

Table 13—Producer losses from price policies and procurement on the wheat, rice, and maize markets, 1965-80

Year	Wheat		Rice		Maize	Wheat, Rice, and Maize	
	Loss from Procurement	Total Loss[a]	Loss from Procurement	Total Loss[a]	Total Loss[a]	Total Loss[a]	Loss Per Metric Ton
	(1975 LE million)						(1975 LE)
1965	15.8	58.2	80.6	171.3	112.5	342.0	66
1966	14.5	48.6	76.7	147.3	91.2	287.1	52
1967	13.6	47.1	93.6	180.6	61.4	289.1	50
1968	12.3	25.9	130.7	243.0	75.7	344.6	54
1969	6.5	33.3	125.0	253.3	86.8	373.4	60
1970	8.9	43.5	63.3	147.2	104.2	294.9	45
1971	10.2	36.9	41.6	98.4	53.2	188.5	29
1972	7.9	32.3	36.5	90.9	61.1	184.3	28
1973	27.7	122.1	76.2	199.5	129.9	415.5	63
1974	40.0	149.4	248.5	725.3	159.2	1,033.9	153
1975	31.2	119.3	261.7	621.1	132.9	873.3	121
1976	17.6	84.4	122.8	295.7	95.8	475.9	65
1977	3.9	27.5	55.0	126.1	13.0	166.6	25
1978	4.1	25.4	65.7	154.7	22.2	202.3	27
1979	13.1	64.8	69.3	143.8	72.7	281.3	38
1980	6.7	72.2	65.3	139.9	15.6	227.7	31

Sources: These figures were computed from data provided by the Egyptian Ministry of Supply, the Central Agency for Public Mobilization and Statistics, and the Principal Bank for Development and Agricultural Investment.

[a] Input subsidies (on fertilizer) are already deducted from total losses.

1980 they amounted to about 10 percent of the total producer losses in the wheat market.

Consumer gains from subsidized government distribution and depressed open market prices have been growing considerably, reaching LE 814 million in 1980. In real per capita terms they were almost twice as high in 1979-80 as they were in the mid-1960s (Table 14). In 1980 farmers contributed 19 percent of the total income transfer to consumers in this market (Appendix 2, Table 35). This means that the implicit subsidy on wheat is about one-fourth of the explicit wheat subsidy that appears in the budget.

The official budget figures for the wheat subsidy are available only for the years after 1970. According to estimates made for this study, wheat subsidies were a significant drain on the government budget even in the mid-1960s (see Table 15).[80] But compared with the subsidies of the 1970s, their effect was small. The model calculations roughly follow the ups and downs of the official series, but differences between 1977 and 1979 are large (see Table 15). In principle, these discrepancies could have arisen either because handling and processing or importing costs were underestimated, or because a different accounting method was used for the official subsidy budget. Mostafa et al. found a similar deviation in a welfare analysis of wheat price policy for 1978/79.[81]

The Rice Market

The rice market was particularly dynamic during the 1960s and 1970s. Production increased remarkably from the mid-1960s to the early 1970s. Exports were at a peak during 1967-70 when the country was particularly short of foreign exchange. Per capita consumption was kept at about 28 kilograms per year during these years as compared to 32-33 kilograms in the late 1970s. When

---

[80] Official exchange rates were used to calculate the budget effects.

[81] See Rasmia Moustafa et al., "A Welfare Analysis of Price Policy for Wheat and Wheat Products in Egypt," Economics Working Paper 48, Agricultural Development Systems Project, Ministry of Agriculture, Cairo, and the University of California-Berkeley, Cairo, 1981.

Table 14—Consumer gains from price policies and subsidies on the wheat, rice, and maize markets, 1965-80

Year	Wheat	Rice	Maize	Aggregate Gain	Per Capita Gain[a]
			(1975 LE million)		(1975 LE)
1965	182.5	109.3	66.2	358.0	12.2
1966	129.7	95.6	40.2	265.5	8.8
1967	134.5	77.2	14.3	226.0	7.4
1968	67.8	105.9	29.4	203.1	6.4
1969	150.5	118.3	40.8	309.6	9.6
1970	183.5	68.5	44.8	296.8	9.0
1971	100.5	49.9	18.9	169.3	5.0
1972	114.9	50.6	24.8	190.3	5.5
1973	394.9	129.4	55.6	579.9	16.4
1974	484.9	515.8	65.0	1,065.7	29.4
1975	375.8	445.1	54.1	875.0	23.6
1976	309.8	240.7	33.0	583.5	15.4
1977	190.4	104.6	10.6	305.6	7.9
1978	236.7	137.1	−4.9	368.9	9.2
1979	375.5	115.6	25.1	516.2	12.6
1980	438.0	118.9	6.8	563.7	13.4

Sources: These figures were computed from data provided by the Egyptian Ministry of Supply, the Central Agency for Public Mobilization and Statistics, and the Principal Bank for Development and Agricultural Investment.

[a] Total population is the denominator used to calculate this column.

Table 15—Changes in the budget caused by government intervention in the wheat, rice, and maize markets, 1965-80

Year	Wheat		Rice[a]	Maize		Total[a]
	Model	Official		Model	Official	
			(1975 LE million)			
1965	21.3	...	14.5	1.2	...	7.8
1966	14.8	...	−18.8	−0.4	...	−4.4
1967	20.3	...	−27.4	−1.9	...	−9.1
1968	−5.6	...	−36.7	0.0	...	−42.3
1969	−5.4	...	−26.9	−0.1	...	−21.6
1970	5.9	21.1	−4.3	0.4	1.1	2.0
1971	0.7	...	−1.8	−0.1	...	−1.2
1972	3.0	19.2	−1.4	0.4	0.6	2.0
1973	131.3	96.1	−16.2	1.8	5.4	116.9
1974	196.4	237.5	−33.0	18.3	18.1	181.7
1975	142.9	260.9	−3.7	14.2	31.1	153.4
1976	80.1	155.6	0.4	9.5	21.0	90.0
1977	38.5	119.9	7.0	7.7	32.7	53.2
1978	59.0	161.3	15.6	−4.7	29.4	69.9
1979	290.1	387.5	−5.6	18.4	35.4	302.9
1980	328.1	274.8	1.9	30.1	20.8	360.1

Sources: The official figures are from Harold Alderman, Joachim von Braun, and Sakr Ahmed Sakr, *Egypt's Food Subsidy and Rationing System: A Description*, Research Report 34 (Washington, D.C.: International Food Policy Research Institute, 1982), p. 16. The calculations for the model figures for wheat and rice are presented in Appendix 2, Tables 35 and 36.

Notes: The model figures were calculated using the official exchange rate. The official figures are subsidies mentioned in the General Authority for Supply Commodities budget for wheat and flour; figures for 1970 and 1980 refer to 1970/71 and 1980/81.

[a] These figures are from the calculations with the model.

exports were high and the per capita supply low, free market prices in the rural areas soared. This led to a wide gap between procurement prices and fixed consumer prices, on the one hand, and open market producer and consumer prices, on the other. As with wheat, there was often a difference between the fixed consumer prices and market prices for rice in the 1970s. But this gap in rice prices was narrowed during 1979 and 1980, as the gap in wheat prices was not, because fixed consumer prices rose (see Table 16). The rice market was heavily taxed and this did not change significantly even when the quantity exported became smaller in absolute terms and in relation to total foreign exchange earnings. The ratios of producer prices show that rice production was taxed more heavily than wheat production during the observed period.

Figure 12 outlines the structure of the rice market. The rice model calculations are given in Appendix 2, Table 36. The total loss by producers because of the difference between world prices and domestic prices is determined by the loss from procurement (G^p_{prc} in Figure 12), the loss from depressed domestic open market prices (G^p_{fre}), and the income that producers could have gained through reallocation of resources under an international price regime (G^p_{soc}). The greater part of the implicit income transfer to consumers is identical with the gain from subsidized rice distribution (G^c_{dis}) and relatively cheap rice on the open domestic market (G^c_{fre}). A lesser part of the consumer gains is financed by the government outlays for procurement below subsidized ration prices. Until 1974, revenues from the implicit export tax were large, but since then the outlays for procurement have often exceeded export revenues (see Table 15).

The income lost by rice producers because of this policy was about LE 260 million in 1980. Subtracting the social loss in production and the small amount of rice export taxes in that year and adding the government outlays for the direct rice subsidy (B^{dis}_{prc}), one

Table 16— Relationship of rice prices to international and open market prices, 1965-80

| | Share of International Price | | | Share of Open Market Price | |
| | Procurement Price | Open Market Producer Price | Fixed Consumer Price[a] | Procurement Price[b] | Fixed Consumer Price[c] |
Year					
	(percent of border price)			(percent of open market price)	
1965	25.7	36.3	32.5	70.7	87.3
1966	23.9	46.7	41.6	51.3	87.0
1967	32.4	51.2	60.7	63.2	86.3
1968	28.5	51.7	48.0	55.0	91.1
1969	29.1	40.0	38.2	72.8	93.3
1970	40.5	51.8	51.3	78.3	96.4
1971	48.6	60.8	60.3	79.9	96.0
1972	49.7	60.0	59.4	82.8	96.2
1973	28.6	37.0	34.8	77.1	91.2
1974	10.8	13.7	12.0	78.8	84.8
1975	14.9	16.5	13.0	90.5	76.4
1976	27.9	29.1	22.2	95.8	74.1
1977	41.8	48.2	34.4	86.7	69.1
1978	42.9	45.9	31.1	93.4	66.0
1979	43.3	49.2	42.5	88.1	83.9
1980	42.0	46.4	39.0	90.5	81.5

Sources: These figures were computed from data provided in 1982 by the Egyptian Ministry of Agriculture, the Central Agency for Public Mobilization and Statistics, and the Ministry of Supply.

Note: The border price is calculated from values of exports, with marketing and processing costs added and corrections made to account for the overvaluation of the currency.

[a] These are in paddy equivalents.

[b] The procurement price is expressed as a percentage of the open market producer price.

[c] The fixed consumer price is expressed as a percentage of the open market consumer price.

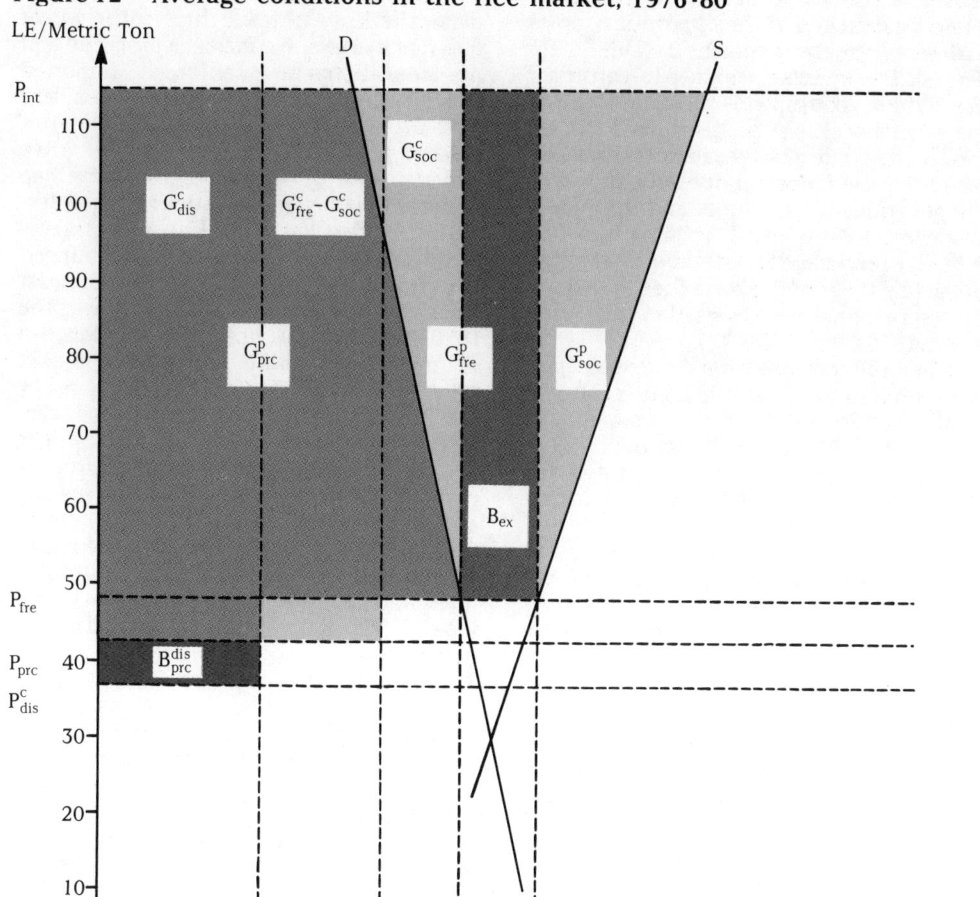

Sources: Calculated from data provided by the Egyptian Ministries of Agriculture and Supply and the Principal Bank for Development and Agricultural Investment.

Notes: Prices are deflated by the consumer price index (1975 = 100). B^{dis}_{prc} is the increase in the government budget caused by procuring and distributing rice, and B_{ex} is the budget revenue from procured rice that is exported. P_{int} is the international price, P_{fre} is the open market price, P_{prc} is the government procurement price, and P^c_{dis} is the fixed consumer price. Q_{ex} is exports from government procurement ($Q_{ex} = Q_{prc} - Q_{dis}$), Q_{prc} is government procurement, Q_{prd} is domestic production (total), Q_{dis} is government distribution ($Q_{prc} + Q_{ex}$), and Q_{dem} is total consumption. S is supply; D is demand.

G^p_{prc} is the producers' loss from government procurement, G^p_{fre} is the producers' loss from depression of the free market price, and G^p_{soc} is the net social loss in production. G^c_{dis} is the consumers's gain from the distribution of rice, G^c_{fre} is the consumers' gain from reduced free market prices, and G^c_{soc} is misallocation in consumption. For further details see Appendix 2.

arrives at the actual subsidy to rice consumers calculated at the opportunity costs to the economy (see Appendix 2, Table 36, for details). This invisible producer-to-consumer rice subsidy corresponds to 20 percent of the official (explicit) budget subsidy for all food commodities, but because it is financed mainly by the farmers it does not appear in the government's accounts and the public awareness of it is small. Income transfers from rice producers to consumers were high in the late 1960s and, except for the years of the international price crisis, they decreased in the 1970s (see Table 13).

The producer loss from depressed open market prices was nearly as high as the loss from compulsory deliveries and sometimes even higher. In the late 1970s the income lost through procurement accounted for about one-third of the total producer losses on the rice market.

Finally, the results indicate that income was forgone because of policy-induced inefficiencies in allocating fewer resources for rice production, which amounted to 13 percent of the total income loss of rice producers in 1980 (see Appendix 2, Table 36). The heavy implicit rice taxation and its allocation effects are not distributed at all equally but they contribute to the disparity of the implicit tax structure between regions and thus to regional differences in farm income. Rice production is concentrated in the northern Nile Delta.[82]

The Maize Market

Maize is the largest cereal crop in Egypt and has shown the greatest expansion since the mid-1960s. Human consumption of maize declined both in per capita terms and in total quantities. It is used mostly as animal feed. Imports of maize, which are also growing, are almost entirely channeled to poultry and livestock producers. The domestic maize crop is of the white variety, whereas yellow maize is imported.

Government's interference in the maize market is less stringent than in the wheat and rice markets. No maize is procured and no area allotment is enforced. Imported maize is distributed by a quota system at a subsidized price. The gap between this subsidized price and the international price widened during the 1970s, while the gap between the open market price and the international price has shrunk in recent years (see Table 17). The open market price ranged between 13 and 57 percent below the border price equivalent at the farm gate during the 1970s, and the subsidized price was between 10 and 55 percent below the open market price (or between 34 and 75 percent below the international price). Maize producers lose income from depressed domestic prices and inefficiency of resource allocation as compared with international prices (see G^p_{fre} and G^p_{soc} in Figure 13). However, the latter is true only if nothing but the price of maize changed. If all commodities were sold at international prices, maize production would lose its current strong advantage and would decline (see the model scenarios in Chapter 3). This means the supply curve (S) in Figure 13 would shift to the left and the slope of the implicit supply curve might be negative.[83]

Part of the income transfer is acquired by maize consumers (G^c_{fre}) but livestock producers also gain ($G^p_{fre} - G^c_{fre}$). Therefore, the producer loss is largely an intrasectoral transfer, and if maize producers are also livestock producers, it is merely an intrafarm transfer. These issues will be addressed in the feed and meat market analysis below.

The subsidy to the maize market is established by the government's import and distribution scheme for using maize for feeding purposes. It amounted to LE 64 million in 1980/81.[84] Other than the implicit consumer subsidy for maize, this explicit subsidy is an income transfer to livestock producers. Its net effect on sector income depends on the effect of this additional maize supply and the meat price policy on meat production.

---

[82] In 1980, 82 percent of the rice area was in the governorates of Kafr-el-Sheikh, Behera, Gharbia, and Sharkia in the northern Delta.

[83] Figure 13 contains a positively sloped implicit supply curve (S), which holds for a separate maize price change rather than a change of all prices. As a result, the net social loss in production appears positive in the figure, whereas it is negative in the empirical results.

[84] Alderman, von Braun, and Sakr, *Egypt's Food Subsidy and Rationing System*, p. 16.

Table 17—Relationship of maize prices to international and open market prices, 1965-80

Year	Open Market Producer Price	Fixed Consumer Price	Fixed Consumer Price as a Share of the Open Market Price
	(percent of border price)		(percent)
1965	41.7	. . .	. . .
1966	52.1	. . .	. . .
1967	63.4	. . .	. . .
1968	54.4	. . .	. . .
1969	54.0	. . .	. . .
1970	50.7	43.0	84.7
1971	59.8	58.9	89.8
1972	63.5	51.9	81.7
1973	48.4	34.4	71.1
1974	43.3	25.6	59.2
1975	44.7	26.4	59.1
1976	51.8	31.0	59.8
1977	81.3	36.9	45.4
1978	78.8	66.2	84.0
1979	59.5	48.0	80.6
1980	87.4	42.7	48.9

Sources: These figures were computed from data provided in 1982 by the Egyptian Ministry of Agriculture, the Central Agency for Public Mobilization and Statistics, and the Ministry of Supply.

Notes: No data on fixed prices before 1970 are available. The border price is calculated from the values of imports, with marketing and processing costs added and corrections made to account for the overvaluation of the currency.

Maize consumers also gain from the imports indirectly, because it leads to reduced domestic maize prices. Imported yellow maize and domestic white maize may be freely substituted for each other in livestock feeding. Both sell at roughly the same price in the open market.[85]

The links between markets for maize are particularly strong. Policies affecting competitive cereals, and all livestock policy as well, affect the maize market. Thus, the conclusions from a partial analysis such as this are limited.

Income and Budget Effects on the Cereal Markets

How cereal market policy affects agriculture becomes clearer when wheat, rice, and maize are aggregated. Excluding the exceptional years of the world food crisis (1973-75), the trend of real income losses of cereal producers has declined significantly since 1965. Cereal production was taxed much less during the second half of the 1970s than in the 1960s. The income loss per ton of cereals in 1975 prices dropped from an average of LE 56 during 1965-69 to LE 30 in 1977-80 (see Table 13). In other words, taxation of cereal production was reduced while explicit food subsidies were increasing dramatically. The parallel development of subsidies and taxation of production, which was so striking during the first half of the 1970s, was not the result of a stable causal relationship between the two. Price policies for consumers and domestic producers were hardly responsive to international price changes.[86] The taxation of cereal production declined in the late 1970s mainly because both rice procurement prices and maize prices increased. Wheat price policy did not have much effect on aggregate cereal prices. Despite the decreased burden on cereal production, implicit income transfers from producers were still LE 422 million in 1980, which corresponds to about 75 percent of the explicit cereal subsidy budget in that year. Rice alone accounted for about 54 percent of that.

Consumers received growing support through depressed cereal prices and subsidized distribution in the late 1970s after several years of reduced transfers following the international food price crisis (see Table 14). In 1980, 78 percent of all consumer gains on cereal markets came from wheat, 21 percent from rice, and 1 percent from maize.

Pulse Markets

Pulses (beans and lentils) are a major source of protein in the Egyptian diet, particularly of the rural and urban poor. However, they are considered an inferior food by

---

[85] These observations were made during market surveys in 1981/82 in rural and urban areas. Subsidized yellow maize is sometimes resold on the open market. Recently some yellow maize has been grown in Fayum.

[86] This finding is also evident from Scobie's study on Egyptian wheat policy (Scobie, *Government Policy and Food Imports*).

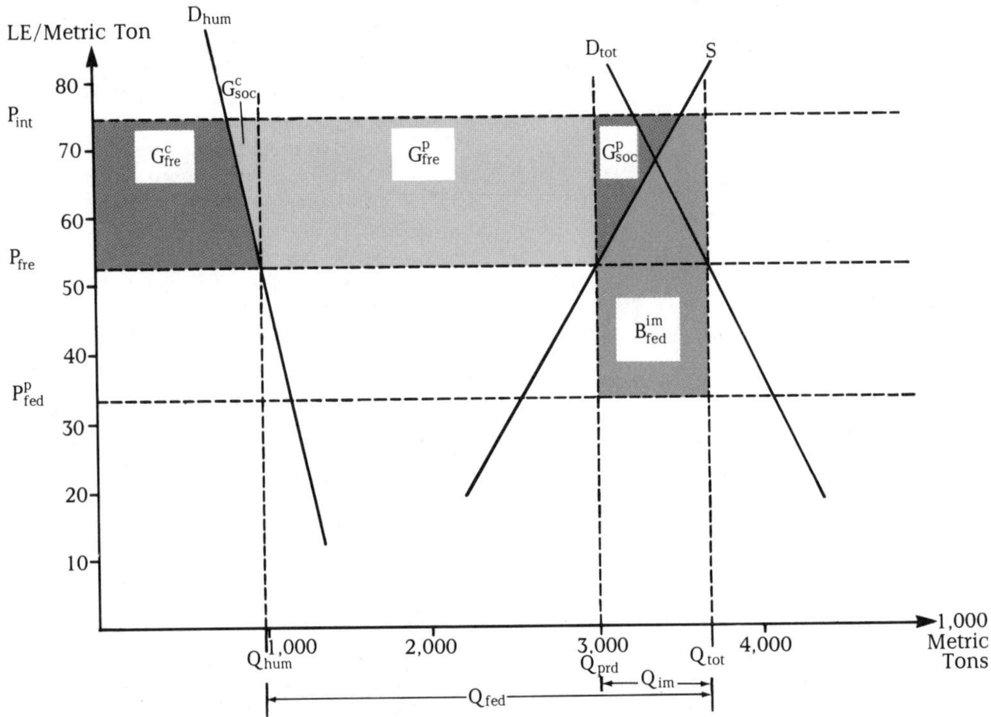

Sources: Calculated from data provided by the Egyptian Ministries of Agriculture and Supply.

Notes: Prices are deflated by the consumer price index (1975=100). B^{im}_{fed} is the increase in the government's budget caused by the subsidized distribution of maize imports. (It includes G^p_{soc} in this figure.) D_{hum} is the demand for maize for food; D_{tot} is the total demand for maize. P_{fre} is the open market price, P_{int} is the international price, and P^p_{fed} is the fixed producer price of maize used as feed.

Q_{fed} is maize used as feed, Q_{hum} is maize used as food, Q_{im} is imports, Q_{prd} is total domestic production, and Q_{tot} is the total supply of white and yellow maize. S is supply.

G^c_{fre} is the consumers' gain from reduced free market prices, and G^c_{soc} is misallocation in consumption. G^p_{fre} is the producers' loss from the depression of the free market price. (The producers' loss also includes G^c_{fre} and G^c_{soc} in this figure.) G^p_{soc} is the net social loss in production.

many.[87] Thus the growth of income may have helped reduce total and per capita consumption of pulses since the mid-1960s.

The procurement prices of beans and lentils were kept at between 50 and 60 percent of international prices during the second half of the 1970s. This reduced the crop's comparative advantage over berseem and other winter crops, and shrank domestic supply, which was only partly balanced by government-controlled imports. These imports and compulsory deliveries from domestic production were channeled into the subsidized distribution system. The decreased total supply caused open market prices to rise. Subsidized consumer prices dropped even further below domestic open market prices than procurement prices did (Table 18).

Because domestic production shrank the total income loss of producers decreased in real terms. During the period 1977-80 the loss per ton of pulses was also reduced. This was mainly because open market prices rose,

---

[87] For urban middle- and high-income groups, negative expenditure elasticities are estimated, whereas urban poor and rural households show relatively high positive elasticities. See von Braun, "A Demand System for Egypt," p. 5.

Table 18—Relationship of bean prices to international and open market prices, 1965-80

Year	Share of International Price			Share of Open Market Price	
	Procurement Price	Open Market Producer Price	Fixed Consumer Price	Procurement Price	Fixed Consumer Price
	(percent of border price)			(percent of open market price)	
1965	. . .	59.3	57.8	. . .	97.8
1966	. . .	58.1	53.5	. . .	91.5
1967	. . .	76.6	64.1	. . .	83.3
1968	. . .	73.8	66.3	. . .	88.6
1969	. . .	60.8	63.1	. . .	96.6
1970	39.4	64.2	61.3	61.3	88.6
1971	43.0	87.2	66.9	49.3	68.3
1972	50.8	81.7	68.4	62.2	74.5
1973	33.7	348.6	43.6	69.3	83.3
1974	38.6	73.3	50.0	52.6	63.9
1975	53.1	71.8	54.7	73.9	72.7
1976	51.6	75.8	53.2	68.1	66.9
1977	47.4	71.9	48.9	65.9	64.9
1978	62.4	85.9	48.4	72.8	53.2
1979	52.3	80.9	40.6	64.7	46.4
1980	55.6	85.3	34.6	65.2	35.7

Sources: These figures were computed from data provided in 1982 by the Egyptian Ministry of Agriculture, the Central Agency for Public Mobilization and Statistics, and the Ministry of Supply.

Notes: No data are available for procurement prices before 1970. The border price is calculated from values of exports, with marketing costs added and corrections made to account for the overvaluation of the currency.

Table 19—Producer losses from price policies and procurement on the beans and lentils markets, 1965-80

Year	Beans		Lentils		Aggregate Loss	Loss Per Metric Ton[a]
	Loss from Procurement	Total Loss	Loss from Procurement	Total Loss		
	(1975 LE million)					(1975 LE)
1965	. . .	32.5	. . .	0.3	32.8	81
1966	. . .	36.8	. . .	3.4	40.2	95
1967	. . .	8.5	. . .	2.1	10.6	48
1968	. . .	14.1	. . .	3.3	17.4	55
1969	. . .	22.4	. . .	3.4	25.8	81
1970	1.3	19.5	. . .	2.4	21.9	71
1971	6.8	10.3	. . .	4.2	14.5	47
1972	5.1	13.3	. . .	5.4	18.7	45
1973	4.1	34.7	. . .	27.9	62.6	187
1974	3.4	13.4	. . .	14.5	27.9	98
1975	4.3	16.1	2.3	10.7	26.8	98
1976	5.2	15.0	3.3	8.4	23.4	80
1977	5.2	17.3	1.7	2.8	20.1	68
1978	2.3	6.6	0.3	0.6	7.2	29
1979	6.2	12.0	0.4	0.5	12.5	51
1980	4.8	8.6	0.5	0.7	9.3	41

Sources: Computed from data provided by the Egyptian Ministries of Agriculture and Supply, the Principal Bank for Development and Agricultural Investment, and the Central Agency for Public Mobilization and Statistics.

Notes: No data on procurement of beans before 1970 are available; no data on procurement of lentils before 1975 are available.

[a] These are given in beans equivalent. Lentils are weighted with a factor of 1.2 to adjust for the average value difference (the average open market price is used as a point of reference).

not because procurement policy changed (see Tables 18 and 19). Total consumer gains from subsidized distribution and depressed domestic open market prices remained high during the 1970s (see Table 20). As lentils received a higher per unit subsidy than beans, absolute consumer gains from both commodities were about the same despite the smaller quantity of lentils consumed.

Pulse market policy appears to be similar to cereal policy. Taxation was far higher than its long-term average in the mid-1970s because only small fractions of international price increases were transmitted to the domestic market. Implicit taxation decreased in the late 1970s because supplies on the open market were tightened, which pressed prices upward, and not because government policy was actively changed.

Current price policy has an important effect on domestic production of pulses. The sector modeling scenarios indicate that pulse production might increase significantly if domestic prices equalled world prices, as current price ratios greatly favor berseem and vegetables, pulses' major competitors (see Chapter 3). The increased share of berseem among those crops grown before cotton shows this.

To sum up, policies in the pulses market are quite similar to those in the wheat market, except that procurement is still compulsory. It is characterized by a consistently wide gap between international and procurement prices, and by a growing gap between procurement and open market prices. The potential effects on production of a streamlined price regime indicate that current policy creates large inefficiencies in the allocation of land for pulses.

The Sugar Market

Egypt was one of the first countries to grow sugarcane and led the trade in sugar until the 16th century. Since then, the sugar industry has flourished in some periods and gone bankrupt in others.[88] Before the construction of the Aswan High Dam, sugar production was largely affected by fluctuating water availability. Since then the regulated water supply has permitted major, stable area expansion. Ninety percent of all sugarcane is grown in the three Upper Egyptian governorates of Menia, Qena, and Asyut. Sugarcane is the major cash crop in this region where no land is allocated to cotton in the government area allotment scheme. About 235,000 feddan, representing 27 percent of the area of these three governorates, is sown with sugarcane.

The state holds a monopoly as miller and trader of cane and sugar. Except for a small quantity of privately processed cane, mainly used for juice, cane is delivered to the state mills. Growers are tied by contracts to one of the seven operating factories. In recent years sugar beet production has been promoted in the northern Nile Delta, but only insignificant amounts were produced during the period studied.

Sugar production has almost doubled since the mid-1960s. Egypt became a net importer of sugar in the 1970s, although net exports occurred in some years until 1973.

Few world agricultural markets are as unstable as the sugar market. And in none have more attempts been made to achieve domestic stability. In 6 out of the 16 years observed, domestic producer prices of sugar (implicit in the price of sugarcane) exceeded the equivalent world price. In some years during the 1960s the farm-gate equivalent world prices for cane were negative, which implies that the value added for sugar production was negative.[89] Domestic production was protected to maintain farm incomes in a region dependent on the crop and to keep the sugar industry in existence during the trough periods of the price cycles.

Because sugarcane is a nontradable having no international value, production and processing—from cane cultivation to sugar refining—are treated as an integrated activity. Consumers are supplied with rationed sugar at subsidized prices. Additional sugar comes from open (black) markets. The open market sugar price, which is an average of black market and second tier (urban) subsidized prices, clears the highly regulated market. This price was higher than the world price in

---

[88] Klaus Baumgarten, "Zuckerwirtschaft in Ägypten" [Sugar Economy in Egypt], *Zuckerindustrie* 104 (September 1979): 854-859.

[89] This finding is in line with calculations from Cuddihy, *Agricultural Price Management in Egypt,* p. 106.

Table 20—Consumer gains from price policies on the beans and lentils markets, 1965-80

Year	Beans	Lentils	Total
		(1975 LE million)	
1965	16.7	0.1	16.7
1966	13.6	2.3	15.9
1967	7.0	2.8	9.8
1968	7.0	4.2	11.2
1969	10.7	6.2	16.9
1970	8.7	3.8	12.5
1971	5.3	3.3	8.6
1972	5.0	4.3	9.3
1973	16.8	11.1	27.9
1974	9.7	10.8	20.5
1975	18.5	18.0	36.5
1976	15.3	18.3	33.6
1977	12.2	9.5	21.7
1978	6.2	5.0	11.2
1979	12.7	8.6	21.3
1980	11.3	12.1	23.4

Sources: Computed from data provided by the Egyptian Ministries of Agriculture and Supply, the Principal Bank for Development and Agricultural Investment, and the Central Agency for Public Mobilization and Statistics.

14 out of the 16 years observed.[90] The sugar price of the basic ration was kept nominally constant during the entire period; the difference between the fixed and open consumer price grew and ranged from 20 to 70 percent between 1965 and 1980 (see Table 21).

As world prices were particularly unstable, only long-term observations of price policy effects make sense for the sugar market. As the time series in Table 22 indicates, the income losses of producers when world prices were high far exceeded the implicit gains of producers when prices were low. In fact, calculated in constant prices, the implicit gains of producers were only 10 percent of their total losses during the entire period 1965-80.

Consumer gains from the subsidized rationed distribution were offset in several years by open market sugar prices, which were frequently higher than world prices. Price policy stabilized the domestic market, and part of the government budget requirements for this policy was provided by revenues generated during periods of low international sugar prices.

The Cotton Market

Because the cotton market has been intensively researched, a description of the policy goals underlying cotton export taxation and the instruments applied may seem redundant.[91] Cotton is included in this analysis, however, because it must compete with the major food crops for production resources. It is sometimes argued that food subsidies increase government expenditures, which are financed by increasing taxation of agriculture, with cotton traditionally ranking first as a crop to be used as a vehicle for indirect taxation.

Cotton production decreased significantly during the 1970s (see Chapter 3). The decline in production and the increase in domestic consumption have reduced exports to almost half of what they were in the mid-1960s. But cotton is still the most important agricultural export commodity.

The entire crop is delivered by the farmers to state collection points. Cotton prices, which are set by a Higher Council with members from several ministries, vary by grade and variety.[92]

Average procurement prices ranged between 20 and 50 percent of the international equivalent during the 1960s and 1970s. The international equivalent for the farm-gate price of seed cotton is calculated from the export unit values of cotton lint, which are converted into seed cotton quantities; marketing and processing costs are subtracted from them; the value of by-products is added; and then the values are corrected for the foreign exchange bias in cotton lint and cottonseed prices.

Much of Egypt's cotton crop is of the extra-long staple type. On the average Egypt produced 43 percent of the world supply of

---

[90] The price series was made available by CAPMAS. For a description of the complex sugar distribution regulations see Alderman, von Braun, and Sakr, *Egypt's Food Subsidy and Rationing System,* p. 34.

[91] See Hansen and Nashashibi, *Foreign Trade Regimes and Economic Development,* p. 206.

[92] For a description of how cotton price policy is administered, see Cuddihy, *Agricultural Price Management in Egypt,* p. 85.

Table 21 — Relationship of sugar prices to international and open market prices, 1965-80

Year	Domestic Cane Price in Sugar Equivalents	Fixed Consumer Price	Open Market Consumer Price	Fixed Consumer Price as a Proportion of the Open Market Consumer Price
	(percent of border price)			(percent)
1965	28.8	94.9	118.6	80.0
1966	105.8	389.1	486.4	80.0
1967	. . .[a]	. . .[a]	. . .[a]	83.3
1968	. . .[a]	. . .[a]	. . .[a]	83.3
1969	66.2	217.9	260.3	83.7
1970	49.2	161.8	258.1	62.9
1971	443.9	1,515.0	2,333.3	64.9
1972	94.8	290.7	450.6	64.5
1973	28.2	70.1	115.7	60.6
1974	15.3	21.9	61.2	35.8
1975	26.8	32.8	87.9	37.3
1976	51.5	56.4	155.0	36.4
1977	87.1	97.8	275.7	35.5
1978	140.9	144.1	435.2	33.3
1979	106.6	98.0	259.3	37.8
1980	41.2	29.2	102.1	28.6

Sources: Computed from data provided by the Egyptian Ministry of Agriculture and the Central Agency for Public Mobilization and Statistics.

Note: The border price is calculated from values of imports, with marketing and processing costs and corrections made to account for the overvaluation of the currency.

[a] In these years the border price of sugar was negative.

that type during 1970-77.[93] Although this gives Egypt the ability to influence the export price of the commodity somewhat, extra-long staple cotton prices are hardly independent from long staple cotton prices in the world market.[94] However, to the extent that Egypt is able to maximize total foreign exchange revenues from cotton trade by imposing an optimum tariff from a quasi-monopoly position, distortion-free prices are overestimated, if the actual export prices are used as a point of reference. The withholding of large amounts of cotton from export in the early 1980s seems to support the hypothesis that Egypt at least tries to influence its export price. But cotton may have been withheld because prices were expected to rise, or because of management problems. Without suitable data, and with some reservations, the analysis here proceeds under the small-country assumption.

Cotton consumption is defined as the quantity acquired by domestic cotton industries.[95] It has grown significantly. Delivery prices to public-sector factories, which are set below procurement prices, further protect the cotton industry.[96] Due to shrinking exports, the highest share of the income transfer from producers is no longer a contribution to the general budget, as it was until 1974. Instead it covers an implicit subsidy (G_{dis}^c) of domestic consumers, which amounted to LE 474 million in 1980.

Input subsidies are of major importance for cotton because the subsidies on pesticides are high. They are considered in the cal-

[93] John M. Page, *Shadow Prices for Trade Strategy and Investment Planning in Egypt,* World Bank Staff Working Paper 521 (Washington, D.C.: World Bank, 1982), p. 100.

[94] Long staple cotton prices act as a floor for the extra-long grade's price. Long and extra-long staple prices show highly correlated price developments.

[95] Cuddihy uses this definition in *Agricultural Price Management in Egypt,* pp. 86-90.

[96] About LE 80 million were allocated for this purpose in the 1981/82 budget.

Table 22—Gains and losses of producers and consumers on the sugar market, 1965-80

Year	Producer Gain or Loss	Consumer Gain or Loss
	(1975 LE million)	
1965	−57.4	41.0
1966	0.5	−39.6
1967	21.5	−66.4
1968	24.9	−55.0
1969	−15.3	−3.8
1970	−29.9	−6.0
1971	18.1	−53.9
1972	−2.6	−38.8
1973	−95.2	56.5
1974	−345.8	218.3
1975	−179.1	153.9
1976	−58.8	24.7
1977	−4.1	−39.5
1978	19.1	−81.8
1979	6.9	−16.2
1980	−90.6	125.6

Sources: Computed from data provided by the Egyptian Ministry of Agriculture and the Central Agency for Public Mobilization and Statistics.

Note: Positive numbers are gains; negative numbers are losses.

culation of farm income loss. Income transfers from producers fluctuated between LE 350 and LE 700 million during the 1970s. The average income transfer per ton of raw cotton measured in deflated prices was somewhat higher in the second half of the 1970s than in the second half of the 1960s, but in 1979-80 there was a significant drop in the implicit taxation of production (see Table 23). This was because domestic output prices rose and input subsidies increased. The total income loss of producers was LE 593 million in 1980.

Cotton producer price policy is largely determined by income support objectives. Prices are set on the basis of the cost of production and a mark-up felt to be adequate for a target farm income.[97] Little adjustment of domestic prices to world prices is made. Hence, the extreme taxation of the cotton crop during 1974-77 was mainly an effect of high international prices while domestic prices remained more or less stable. However, budget revenue considerations might have caused this low transmission elasticity. This will be analyzed more comprehensively with particular reference to food subsidies later. At this point, it is worth noting that when government outlays for food subsidies were exploding during 1973-80, there were two distinct price policies for cotton: extremely high taxation during the first period (1974-77) and moderate to low taxation—if measured against standards of the 1960s and early 1970s—during the following period (1978-80). No obvious relation between the taxation of cotton and the increase in budgetary needs because of increased subsidy outlays is apparent.

The important by-product of cotton production—cottonseed cake—is taken into account in the feed market analysis in the next chapter.

Animal Produce Markets and Feed

Egypt's livestock density is one of the highest in the world. Its animal production sector is closely linked to all cropping activities because cattle and buffalo are used as draft animals and because fodder production and fodder by-products of major crops are important. Because almost no range land is available in the country, the opportunity cost of fodder is determined by the prices of all other crops. The following analysis focuses on the red meat and milk markets and the policies affecting the output and input prices of these commodities. The fast-growing poultry sector is included in the feed policy analysis.

Red Meat

A detailed analysis of the implications of price policy for the Egyptian meat market is impaired by insufficient data.[98] Because

---

[97] See Saad Nassar, M. R. el-Amir, and A. A. Moustafa, "Determinants of Agricultural Price Policy in Egypt," Economics Working Paper 50, Agricultural Development Systems Project, Ministry of Agriculture, Cairo, and the University of California-Berkeley, Cairo, 1982, p. 12.

[98] James B. Fitch and Ibrahim Soliman, "The Livestock Economy in Egypt: An Appraisal of the Current Situation," Cairo, 1982 (mimeographed).

	Producer Loss		
Year	Aggregate	Loss Per Metric Ton	Consumer Gain[a]
	(1975 LE million)	(LE)	(1975 LE million)
1965	528.8	328	139.8
1966	390.8	278	70.0
1967	311.8	231	75.9
1968	357.3	265	105.5
1969	600.8	361	213.5
1970	550.5	353	164.1
1971	473.8	302	120.4
1972	448.5	284	143.4
1973	505.0	343	150.1
1974	805.5	617	192.2
1975	606.5	532	161.9
1976	473.4	406	157.4
1977	605.0	514	170.6
1978	369.2	311	151.4
1979	266.2	207	188.2
1980	319.2	228	187.8

Sources: Computed from data provided by the Egyptian Ministry of Agriculture and the Central Agency for Public Mobilization and Statistics.

[a] Calculated for the cotton industry on the basis of the government's delivery price of cotton to factories.

production statistics are based on crude estimates, the analytical results should be interpreted cautiously. The meat analysis in this report focuses on cattle and buffalo meat. Sheep, goats, and camels, which supply about 15 percent of all red meat produced, are not dealt with here. Ministry of Agriculture meat production figures show that the number of sheep, goats, and camels showed a slight tendency to grow in the 1970s. Despite rapidly increasing imports, the growth of total supply of red meat was only modest, which, as income growth and the income elasticities of meat demand were high, led to a tremendous rise in prices during the 1970s. The consumer price index of meat products rose to 428 between 1970/71 and 1980/81, and the cost-of-living price index rose to 252.[99] The index of farm-gate prices of beef rose to 369 (also see the border price equivalents given in Appendix 1, Table 34).

Since the mid-1970s domestic meat prices have exceeded international prices, which indicates that meat production is protected. Although private meat imports have been permitted in principle since the mid-1970s, they are still small. This does not seem plausible at first glance. With domestic prices higher than import prices, importing meat should be profitable. But import license restrictions, the importers' lack of foreign exchange, and controls on the marketing margins of importers, calculated on the basis of the official exchange rate, have discouraged private imports and contributed to protectionism. Another constraint on private imports is the lack of privately owned refrigerated transport and distribution facilities. Thus the Ministry of Supply's foreign purchasing decision remains the determinant of import quantities. The Ministry uses numerous instruments to influence domestic meat production and distribution. Among these are the compulsory delivery of meat produced with subsidized feed (1979/80) and restriction of sales of retail meat to three days of the week.

Government frozen meat imports are sold in portions at a subsidized fixed price that is less than both the import and domestic open market prices.[100] The basic features of the beef market in the late 1970s are described in Figure 14. It demonstrates that consumers lose in open market purchases (G^c_{fre}) whereas they gain from the distribution of subsidized imports by the government (G^c_{dis}).

Livestock production in Egyptian agriculture rarely serves just one purpose. Most meat and milk is produced from draft animals kept on small family farms. This means that high meat (and milk) prices are an indirect incentive for continuing to use draft animals instead of machinery using diesel or electrical power.[101] The dual uses for cattle and buffalo also explain why domestic meat production

---

[99] The consumer price index refers to meat, fish, and eggs (CAPMAS, 1982).

[100] See Alderman, von Braun, and Sakr, *Egypt's Food Subsidy and Rationing System,* for a description of the system of subsidized meat distribution to consumers.

[101] Note that energy is subsidized too, which somewhat offsets the distortion in favor of draft animals.

Figure 14—Average conditions in the beef market, 1976-80

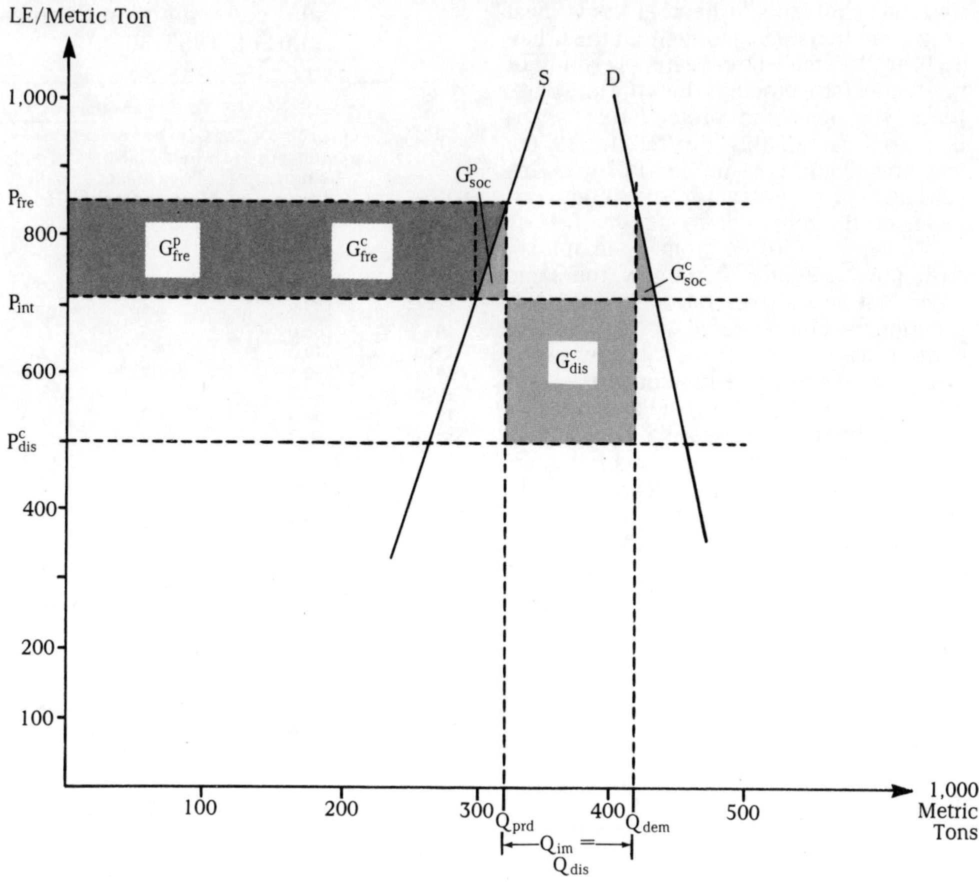

Sources: Calculated from data provided by the Egyptian Ministries of Agriculture and Supply.

Notes: Prices are deflated by the consumer price index (1975 = 100). P_{int} is the international price, P_{fre} is the open market price, and P_{dis}^c is the fixed consumer price. Q_{prd} is domestic production (total), Q_{dis} is government distribution, Q_{dem} is total consumption, and Q_{im} is imports (= $Q_{dem} - Q_{prd}$). S is supply; D is demand. G_{fre}^p is the producers' gain from the free market price, and G_{soc}^p is the net social loss in production. G_{dis}^c is the consumer's gain from the distribution of subsidized beef, G_{fre}^c is the consumers' loss from protected free market prices, and G_{soc}^c is misallocation in consumption. For further details see Appendix 2.

has not been able to keep pace with demand despite the high price increases. As the high feed/meat conversion rates indicate, the marginal productivity of fodder used for increased meat output is low partly because of the genetic characteristics of the local breeds. Nevertheless, the growth in fodder production during the 1970s indicates that the price structures gave farmers a strong incentive to expand livestock production. The modeling exercise demonstrates that Egyptian agriculture has no real comparative advantage in livestock production, given the high opportunity costs of land and, in the long run, of water (see Chapter 3).

Because meat is consumed mainly by the high-income population, the price policy has important implications for equity as well. The income transfer calculations discussed below should be seen in this light. About 50 percent of all meat products are consumed by the high- and middle-income urban population, which is 31 percent of the total population.[102] In other words, meat protection transfers income from the urban (rich) to the small-farm sector. Taxation of most other farm products does the opposite. Farmers' gains from protectionist prices increased remarkably during the 1970s, reaching about LE 41 million in 1980. This partially compensates for the producers' losses on the other commodity markets.

Consumers' losses from open market meat purchases are of roughly the same order. But subsidized, rationed meat distribution has compensated for a larger share of these losses in recent years, because subsidized meat prices are nominally constant (see Table 24). Most subsidized meat is channeled into urban areas.[103] This implies that the high open market prices for meat, which favor producers in rural areas mainly at the cost of urban consumers, are somewhat balanced by the government's subsidy and rationing program. The subsidy budget for beef is calculated at about LE 57 million for 1980 (see Appendix 2, Table 37). It has grown quickly in recent years.

Milk

Egypt's milk market is flourishing in obscurity. Statistical information on production is vague and based on estimates rather than on surveys.[104] According to statistics of the Ministry of Agriculture, production increased steadily during the 1970s by about 1.5 percent per year. Milk is mainly produced on small and medium family farms. Milk, home-processed butter *(ghee)*, and cheese provide major sources of regular cash income for those farm households producing a marketed surplus. These milk products are marketed either directly by producers or by small peddlers.

The eight government-operated milk plants in the country process about 50,000 tons of fresh milk per year, some of which is sold through government outlets at fixed prices and some of which is marketed by merchants.[105] Public-sector companies are major recipients of imported skimmed milk powder and butter oil. The bulk of these two commodities is delivered to Egypt under food aid terms from the European Community, which in recent years has normally sent about 10,000 tons of milk powder and 3,000 tons of butter oil each year. Of that, in 1980-81, 7,000 tons of milk powder and 2,800 tons of butter oil were used as nonproject

Table 24—Gains and losses of producers and consumers on the meat market, 1965-80

		Consumer	
		Gain or Loss	
	Producer	from Fixed	Total
	Gain or	Price Meat	Gain or
Year	Loss	Distribution	Loss
		(1975 LE million)	
1965	−163.3	18.9	92.6
1966	−152.8	4.9	62.7
1967	−105.0	−1.5	31.6
1968	−40.2	−5.5	−9.1
1969	−60.3	−1.7	21.6
1970	−57.3	−5.9	−5.0
1971	−94.5	−4.3	16.4
1972	−30.2	−12.4	−57.6
1973	−177.1	1.0	64.1
1974	−82.7	2.0	1.4
1975	18.9	−5.1	−105.1
1976	31.3	−3.0	−162.0
1977	−10.3	12.9	−80.5
1978	20.3	13.2	−100.2
1979	−61.2	33.9	29.1
1980	22.3	42.2	−62.1

Sources: Computed from data provided by the Egyptian Ministries of Agriculture and Supply and the Central Agency for Public Mobilization and Statistics.

Note: Positive numbers are gains; negative numbers are losses.

---

[102] This is calculated on the basis of CAPMAS, *Family Budget Survey, 1974/75.* See von Braun, "A Demand System for Egypt."

[103] See Alderman, von Braun, and Sakr, *Egypt's Food Subsidy and Rationing System,* p. 35.

[104] The most recent representative survey on livestock and animal production available is for 1970. Since then, annual milk production has been estimated on the basis of a projected change of the cattle herd, its assumed age structure, and milk production per head. The milk yields per head used in the calculation for 1979 were for buffalo, old: 1,168 kilograms per year; medium: 899 kilograms per year; and for cows, average: 674 kilograms per year. This unpublished information was provided by the Ministry of Agriculture, Cairo.

[105] This information was obtained from the Misr Dairy Company, Cairo, 1979.

food aid, which means it was processed in the public plants. It is either reconstituted as milk or made into cheese.[106] These imports are exempt from the analysis of the milk market, because they make up only about 4 percent of total consumption (calculated in milk equivalents).

Consumption of milk products in Egypt is not confined to the higher income (urban) population, as it is in many subtropical or tropical countries. The average consumption of milk and milk products in 1975 by rural low-income groups was about 51 kilograms per capita, while the country average was 67 kilograms.[107] Village-made butter and cheese is a major fat and protein component in the diet of the rural poor.

Despite the dietary importance of the commodity, the government intervenes less in the milk market than in other basic food markets. Most of the interventions are in production (for example, the public-sector feed supply, upgrading of local cattle, and veterinary services). Although these may have helped increase domestic milk production, demand seems to have grown faster, which explains rising milk prices. The index of farm-gate prices for milk has increased from 100 to 350 since 1970. This increase, like the increase in meat prices, is far greater than the average increase of consumer prices.

There are particular problems associated with calculating the income transfers and welfare effects on the milk market, because fresh milk is not traded. To measure the shadow price of milk, the unit value of milk powder imports is converted to a liquid milk equivalent and corrected for the distortion in the rate of foreign exchange. Of course, this is an approximation only. Domestic milk prices seem to have been much higher than the equivalent international prices in recent years. In 1980 domestic prices were about 80 percent higher than world prices. The prices were close together until the mid-1970s; the world price exceeded the domestic in some years before that. Since then, international prices have been nominally stable because milk production has been heavily protected in the major milk producing countries, which has led to increases of export surpluses from those countries.

According to estimates based on the world price, Egyptian milk producers gained about LE 200 million in 1980 (see Table 25). Consumer income losses were about LE 370 million in 1980.[108] The net social loss in consumption is rather high as demand for milk is price elastic.

In spite of uncertainties with the data, it is clear that protection of the milk market has increased as domestic prices have risen and world prices have remained nominally stable. Although these developments occurred at the same time that food subsidy expenditures were increasing, no particular causal linkage is evident. However, it is worth noting that implicit income transfers to milk producers, added to those calculated for meat producers, offset a large share of the losses of producers in those markets that are effectively taxed. The ruminants appear to allow producers to compensate for some of the burden depressed prices of cereals, pulses, cotton, and sugar put on their income.

Feed

As stated earlier, price distortions affect not only the distribution of income between producers and consumers but income transfers between crop and livestock production sectors as well. Insofar as feed prices are distorted, they will change the competitiveness of livestock production with crop production. Whether this also implies that income will shift between crop farms and livestock farms depends on the degree of specialization in Egyptian agriculture. Available information suggests that, except for a small but steadily growing specialized poultry sector, livestock production in general and cattle and buffalo production in particular are evenly distributed among farms. Table 38 in Appendix 2 shows the development of stocks in the livestock sector.

About 65 percent of all animals are kept on farms of less than 3 feddan. The value of

---

[106] These statistics were provided by the office of the World Food Programme, Cairo, 1982.

[107] These figures are calculated in cow milk equivalents from CAPMAS, *Family Budget Survey, 1974/75.* See von Braun, "A Demand System for Egypt," p. 47.

[108] Consumer prices are derived from farm-gate price statistics, adding a constant relative markup of 20 percent for marketing costs.

Table 25—Gains and losses of producers and consumers on the milk market, 1965-80

Year	Producer Gain or Loss	Consumer Gain or Loss
	(1975 LE million)	
1965	11.2	−36.5
1966	21.2	−51.6
1967	32.7	−71.4
1968	−91.5	56.9
1969	−115.3	70.3
1970	−70.4	39.3
1971	−48.1	17.5
1972	−134.9	83.9
1973	−40.2	5.1
1974	7.0	−50.6
1975	−32.0	−5.8
1976	−0.3	−50.4
1977	65.3	−137.8
1978	77.5	−157.5
1979	107.7	−203.6
1980	106.4	−198.7

Sources: Computed from data provided by the Egyptian Ministries of Agriculture and Supply and the Central Agency for Public Mobilization and Statistics.

Note: Positive numbers are gains; negative numbers are losses.

animal products on these small farms is nearly as high as the value of crop production.[109] Because the majority of the small farms operate a mixed crop-livestock production pattern, one may assume that most implicit feed subsidies do not have much effect on the distribution of personal income within agriculture. A detailed livestock survey by Soliman et al. indicates that the share of subsidized concentrate feed mix in the total feed supply used is about the same for all sizes of farms.[110]

The implications of feed subsidies for distribution would change if intensive poultry production were to continue to grow, especially near urban areas. These specialized poultry production companies would benefit from the low-priced feed supplies. Yet in 1980 the total feed used to produce poultry and eggs, most of which is still produced under typical small-farm conditions, amounted to just 577,000 tons of starch units. This is not more than 7 percent of total feed demand and approximately 18 percent of the total nutrients in concentrate feed (see Appendix 2, Tables 39 and 40).

Another question needs to be raised about the relationship between feed subsidies and the prices of livestock products. Do feed subsidies benefit consumers by reducing meat prices? Considering the marketing system and the supply-demand situation, this is unlikely to happen as long as Egypt is an importing country where prices are determined mainly by import prices and the tariffs and costs of implicit trade barriers. Actually, the Egyptian government has been trying for some time to have the feed subsidy transmitted to meat prices. Those farmers who receive subsidized feed have been obliged since September 1981 to sell some of the livestock produced with that feed to government slaughterhouses at a low fixed price. Yet frequent observations suggest that these fixed prices for livestock production are seldom enforced. According to calculations presented by Soliman, this should not be surprising, at least insofar as the general price-fixing policy is concerned.[111] Soliman calculates that, under average production conditions, a farmer who receives only the official fixed price for his cattle cannot cover his costs of production if obliged to sell the product at the fixed price. As a result, he may refrain from fattening cattle unless he is able to sell his produce on the open market. Most farmers seem to be doing this.

As a consequence, in the following calculation the subsidy of feed (S) of a certain category (i) is defined as the wedge between national and world prices ($P_i^{int} - P_i^d$), multiplied by the quantity (Q_i) without adjustments for changes of livestock prices induced by subsidies:

[109] Ibrahim Soliman, James B. Fitch, and Nesreen Abdel Aziz, "The Role of Livestock Production on the Egyptian Farm," Economics Working Paper 85, Agricultural Development Systems Project, Ministry of Agriculture, Cairo, and the University of California-Berkeley, Cairo, July 1982, p. 7.

[110] Ibid., pp. 31-32.

[111] Ibrahim Soliman, "Red Meat Price Policy in Egypt," Economics Working Paper 62, Agricultural Development Systems Project, Ministry of Agriculture, Cairo, and the University of California-Berkeley, Cairo, 1982.

$$S_i = Q_i \left(P_i^{int} - P_i^d\right). \qquad (15)$$

The main sources of feed supply in Egypt are berseem and leaves of maize, which provide green fodder; straw; and concentrated feed components, including wheat and rice bran and cottonseed cake. Direct subsidies are being paid to distribute imported maize directly and for the growing amount of feed mix available, which consists of several combinations of bran, imported maize, cottonseed cake, and other, minor ingredients. A comparison of domestic and world prices or price equivalents for the remaining feed categories— namely berseem, but also domestic cottonseed cake, bran, and maize not used in feed mix— reveals that their prices are also distorted. This is obviously not only the result of trade barriers and quotas for these commodities themselves, but also of prices transmitted indirectly from the directly subsidized feed and food categories.

The empirical basis for the computation of feed quantities is provided by the supply-disappearance balances as described in Appendix 2. These balances have been generated using estimates of production, consumption, waste, seed, and stock changes. With the exception of maize and sorghum, where human consumption was reestimated from family budget surveys, most data, including the extraction rates of by-products, are derived from FAO and Ministry of Agriculture sources.

As the data in Appendix 2 indicate, supplies of maize and wheat bran show the highest growth rates. The rapid growth of maize supplies is a consequence of increases of production and, since 1974/75, of imports coupled with a steady decrease in human consumption. According to the extrapolations from family budget surveys, between 1965 and 1980 annual maize consumption declined from 67 to 38 kilograms per capita in rural areas and from 14 to 4 kilograms per capita in urban areas. As a consequence, the share of maize in the total supply of energy from concentrates rose from 50 percent to 75 percent. It is evident that the implicit subsidies on maize strongly affect the feed subsidy.

Sorghum shows a similar pattern. Consumption in animal feed substitutes for that consumed by humans. This explains the strong growth of this feed component, which is mainly used for poultry. The total supply of the other major components of concentrate feed, rice bran and cottonseed cake, was more stagnant, which reflects their decreasing share of total area. Finally, much of the increase in berseem production is a direct reflection of the decline in the area sown with cotton, which enabled long-season berseem to be substituted for short-season berseem.

An aggregation of all major feed categories using starch units as weighting factors, shows that the proportion of concentrates in total feed has been steadily increasing, amounting to nearly 40 percent in 1980 (see Appendix 2, Table 40).[112] While the total supply of energy increased by approximately 50 percent between 1965 and 1980, the supply of energy in concentrates has almost tripled.

An assessment of total feed subsidies can be made from a comparison of the total feed supplies valued at domestic prices with the total supplies valued at world market prices (see Table 26). A major and growing proportion of the government's direct subsidy occurs through the distribution of ready feed mix, which has included a large share of cottonseed cake since the mid-1970s. Therefore, the subsidy on feed mix is calculated separately from the subsidy on the remaining quantities of feed components.

If berseem is included, the total of explicit and implicit subsidies in 1980 came to nearly LE 400 million. Yet the time series using 1975 prices shows a clearly declining trend for subsidies. This is mainly because of the rapid decline of real subsidies implied in the domestic berseem price. The gap between the farm-gate price of berseem and the world price equivalent has been steadily reduced. It is difficult to explain what determines the producer price of berseem, especially since only a small proportion of total production is marketed.[113] The com-

---

[112] Starch units are chosen because energy is typically a scarce factor in Egyptian feed diets, whereas protein is available in sufficient quantities due to the large amounts of berseem and maize that are fed.

[113] According to survey results, only about 13 percent of the berseem produced is marketed. See Soliman, Fitch, and Aziz, "The Role of Livestock Production," p. 31.

Table 26— Subsidies for selected feed categories and total feed subsidies, 1965-80

Year	Feed Mix	Individual Feeds[a]				Berseem	Total	
		Cotton-seed Cake	Wheat and Rice Bran	Maize	Total		Current Prices	Constant Prices
		(1975 LE million)					(LE million)	(1975 LE million)
1965	15.5	84.2	17.9	46.2	163.8	282.0	287.6	445.8
1966	18.6	78.0	7.5	41.1	145.1	329.2	333.5	474.3
1967	26.0	66.8	4.1	28.4	125.3	314.8	311.6	440.1
1968	20.0	51.0	5.3	36.0	112.4	316.2	299.1	428.5
1969	27.2	70.8	9.7	41.4	149.2	333.0	347.6	482.2
1970	27.6	68.1	11.2	54.2	161.1	354.6	386.2	515.7
1971	29.1	64.8	4.3	24.4	122.5	308.9	333.1	431.5
1972	33.5	62.8	5.5	33.3	135.1	329.9	366.4	465.0
1973	35.8	61.4	12.4	76.5	186.1	219.6	333.5	405.7
1974	32.9	48.8	18.7	124.6	225.0	212.3	398.4	437.3
1975	30.8	9.3	12.2	120.6	172.9	176.6	349.5	349.5
1976	49.6	6.4	14.0	92.1	162.2	209.1	409.6	371.3
1977	53.9	8.5	5.2	36.5	104.2	181.0	354.5	285.2
1978	57.7	3.7	5.5	40.9	107.7	78.4	257.0	186.1
1979	66.1	9.9	4.1	67.6	147.8	79.6	345.2	227.4
1980	93.8	7.1	1.9	41.7	144.5	69.3	397.4	213.8

Source: Computed from data provided by the Egyptian Ministries of Agriculture and Supply and the Central Agency for Public Mobilization and Statistics.

[a] These feeds were not included in the feed mix.

parative advantage of berseem can be seen in the farming system in general. There are indications that factors that increase production may have dampened the price increase. These factors include the steady substitution of long-season berseem for short-season berseem mentioned above and the low opportunity costs of land because competing winter crops, especially wheat, are taxed throughout the period 1965-80. The price of berseem may have increased because both beef prices and the derived demand for ruminant feed did. If berseem is excluded from the feed subsidies, a time series of direct and indirect subsidies on concentrate feed components can be derived. While the sum of these subsidies has been growing in nominal terms, they have been constant in real terms (Table 26). Yet the mix of feeds receiving these subsidies has changed. The subsidies on those feed categories subject to direct government intervention, such as ready feed mix and maize used separately as feed, have grown. But the subsidies on individual feed components not included in ready feed mix have shrunk.

Insofar as the implicit feed subsidies are not just transfers between sectors within agriculture or farms, they affect agricultural income significantly. And insofar as these feed and roughage items are unevenly distributed by types of farms and by regions, the price structure has important implications for the income distribution between sectors and regions. This issue requires further analyses based on farm household production and income information. Direct and indirect feed subsidies, with protectionism on the output side of animal production, give a different picture of the aggregate taxation of agriculture than if only the major field crops are taken into account.

7

THE BURDEN ON AGRICULTURE—DEVELOPMENT AND DETERMINANTS WITH SPECIAL FOCUS ON FOOD SUBSIDIES

The analysis of agricultural policy by commodity in the last chapter made the system seem like a confusing mosaic. This chapter will try to show how the parts of the mosaic fit together. Attempts will be made to explain how the aggregate burden on producers developed and to define its major components. Hypotheses will be tested to find out what policies determine its size and form. And, the way food subsidies change the burden will be analyzed.

Development and Components of the Burden

The aggregate burden on the sector (TB) in year t is the sum of all welfare gains and losses of producers:[114]

$$TB_t = \sum_{i=1}^{10} G_{p,t}^i, \qquad (16)$$

where

$G_{p,t}^i$ = the burden on producers from implicit taxation or protection of commodity i in year t (G_p as defined in equation [7]), and

$i=1,\ldots,10$ = the commodities wheat, rice, maize, beans, lentils, sugar, cotton, meat, milk, and feed.

TB represents the sum of all farm income transferred by government procurement, farmers's open market activities, and subsidized input supplies, and of net losses from the misallocation of resources. This burden, expressed in 1975 prices, fluctuated between LE 500 million and LE 1 billion between 1965 and 1972. After an extraordinary peak in 1973-75 it dropped to about LE 350 million per year in 1976 (see Table 27). In other words, agriculture was implicitly taxed much less in the second half of the 1970s than before.

The total burden was reduced mostly by lowering the burden on cereals and cotton and increasing protection of animal products. It was mainly the development of livestock protection after 1974 that changed the relationship between agriculture and the rest of the economy (see Figure 15).

Table 28 confirms that wheat price policy added little to aggregate taxation. Producer losses in wheat production usually added only 3 to 10 percent to the total burden. Only in recent years, when implicit taxation on that commodity remained stable while the aggregate burden shrank, has wheat's contribution increased. The contribution of maize is also low, though it has fluctuated much more because its domestic prices have been unstable. Rice's contribution has been higher, about 30 to 40 percent in the second half of the 1970s. Cotton's effect on the total burden has been overwhelming. Since the gains from livestock protection and input subsidies have reduced the total burden, the share of cotton has increased. The rapid changes in the livestock market are a major cause of the reduction of the burden since 1974 (Table 28). Without the livestock protection and feed subsidies, the aggregate burden in 1980 would have been 73 percent higher.

The producer burden—the farm income forgone as a consequence of price and market interventions—is determined by several seemingly unrelated factors. Policies on taxation of agriculture, support of farm income, and price policies, which are directed

---

[114] Direct taxation is excluded here. Cuddihy's assumption that this may balance off with the implicit subsidy of free water supply to field borders is followed (Cuddihy, *Agricultural Price Management in Egypt*).

Table 27—Aggregate gains and losses of producers on agricultural commodity markets, 1965-80

Year	Cereals, Pulses, and Sugar	Meat and Milk	Feed[a]	Cotton	Total Burden
		(1975 LE million)			
1965	-432.20	-152.17	163.83	-528.79	-949.34
1966	-326.70	-131.55	145.10	-390.78	-703.94
1967	-278.16	-72.38	125.32	-311.79	-537.01
1968	-337.13	-131.66	112.37	-357.28	-713.70
1969	-414.40	-175.56	149.16	-608.81	-1,041.62
1970	-346.71	-127.76	161.09	-550.49	-863.87
1971	-184.97	-142.66	122.55	-473.76	-678.84
1972	-205.70	-165.10	135.08	-448.49	-684.21
1973	-609.26	-217.37	186.10	-505.04	-1,145.56
1974	-1,407.61	-75.71	225.03	-805.50	-2,063.78
1975	-1,082.17	-13.03	172.95	-606.46	-1,528.72
1976	-558.03	30.91	162.25	-473.44	-838.31
1977	-190.88	54.98	104.19	-605.01	-636.72
1978	-190.32	97.74	107.74	-369.25	-354.09
1979	-286.82	46.56	147.79	-266.15	-358.62
1980	-327.76	128.74	144.46	-319.18	-373.74

Sources: These are aggregated results of partial equilibrium models of the indicated markets calculated from data provided by the Egyptian Ministries of Agriculture and Supply and the Central Agency for Public Mobilization and Statistics.

Notes: Positive numbers are gains; negative numbers are losses.

[a] This excludes berseem. It should be noted that the producer losses computed for the maize market are compensated for by the implicit producer gains from depressed feed maize prices to the extent that domestically produced maize is fed to animals.

toward improving Egypt's self-sufficiency, contribute positively or negatively to the aggregate net burden. The following is an attempt to identify the major determinants of the producer burden, to trace the explanatory variables accounting for its recent rapid decrease, and to assess the effect food subsidies have had on it.

Determinants of the Burden

Because Egyptian policymakers give high priority to stabilizing domestic agricultural prices, and food prices in particular, it seems obvious that instability in international prices would contribute to fluctuations in the producer's burden. So would government interventions in crop allocation, procurement, and input subsidization. Government quotas on imports and exports add to the burden by affecting domestic open market prices. Each of these factors reflects the amount of resources available to the government and the goals set for development and income redistribution. In other words, the government revenues in a given year should be expected to affect the burden on agriculture. Indirect taxation of agriculture is particularly attractive for a government that has problems collecting direct taxes. Indirect taxes through procurement are easier to administer in the short run, especially since procurement prices in Egypt are usually announced shortly before the procurement season begins.

As the time series of the implicit producer-consumer transfers on the major food commodity markets show, explicit food subsidies evolved out of a system of implicit consumer subsidies largely financed by agriculture (see Tables 13, 14, and 15). The skyrocketing budget for the system after 1973 is astonishing only if the implicit subsidies of earlier years are ignored. High population growth, high income growth, and weak performance of agricultural production suddenly induced a rapid decrease in self-sufficiency. How did agricultural policy react?

If stabilizing the prices of subsidized and rationed commodities were a fixed ob-

Figure 15—Producer losses and gains on commodity markets and aggregate net burden, 1965-80

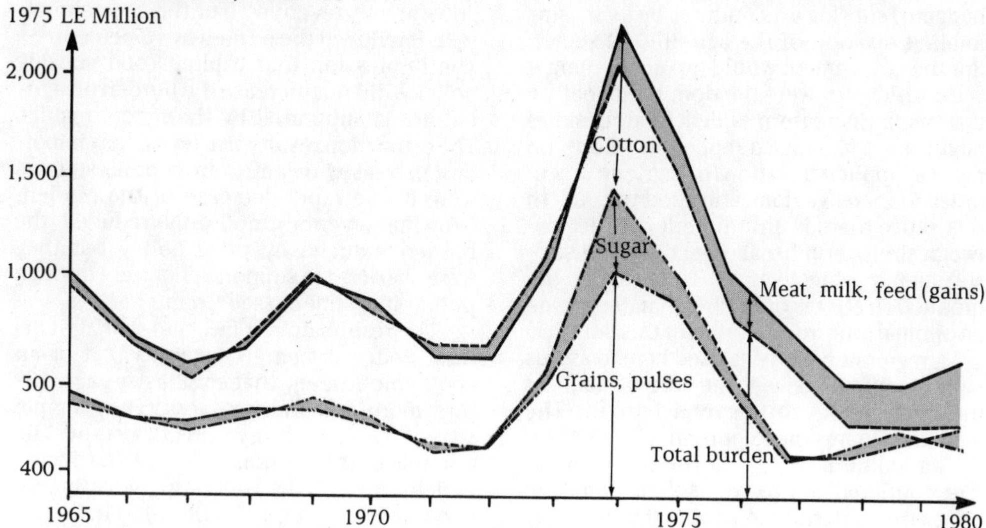

Sources: These are aggregated results of partial equilibrium models of the indicated markets calculated from data provided by the Egyptian Ministries of Agriculture and Supply and the Central Agency for Public Mobilization and Statistics.

Notes: The total burden is the sum of the losses from taxation minus the gains from protection on the markets. The amount a commodity contributes to the burden is the distance between its line and the line below it (not the distance from the horizontal axis, except for grains and pulses). When the shaded area representing the contribution of meat, milk, and feed lies above the total burden line, it shows a gain from meat, milk, and feed (which is deducted from the burden). When that shaded area is below the total burden line, it shows a loss from meat, milk, and feed. Similarly, when the line for sugar is below the line for grains and pulses, the shaded area represents a gain from sugar, and when it is above, it shows a loss from sugar. Grains and pulses and cotton always show losses.

Table 28—Components of the burden on agriculture, 1965-80

Year	Wheat	Maize	Rice	Beans	Lentils	Meat, Milk and Feed	Sugar	Cotton
					(percent)			
1965	6.1	11.2	18.0	3.4	0.3	−1.2	6.0	55.7
1966	6.9	12.9	20.9	5.2	0.4	−1.9	−0.1	55.5
1967	8.7	11.4	33.6	1.5	0.3	−9.8	−3.9	58.0
1968	3.6	10.6	34.0	1.9	0.4	2.7	−3.4	50.2
1969	3.1	8.3	24.3	2.1	0.3	2.5	1.4	57.6
1970	5.0	12.0	17.0	2.2	0.2	−3.8	3.4	63.7
1971	5.4	7.8	14.5	1.5	0.6	2.9	−2.6	69.7
1972	4.7	8.9	13.2	1.9	0.7	4.3	0.3	65.5
1973	10.8	11.3	17.4	3.0	2.4	2.7	8.3	44.0
1974	7.2	7.7	35.1	0.6	0.7	−7.2	16.7	39.0
1975	7.8	8.8	40.6	1.0	0.6	−10.4	11.7	39.6
1976	10.0	11.4	35.2	1.7	0.9	−23.0	7.0	56.4
1977	4.3	2.0	19.7	2.7	0.4	−25.0	0.6	95.0
1978	7.1	6.2	43.6	1.8	0.1	−58.0	−5.3	104.2
1979	18.0	20.2	40.0	3.3	0.1	−54.1	−1.9	74.2
1980	19.3	4.1	37.4	2.3	0.2	−73.0	24.2	85.4

Sources: These are aggregated results of partial equilibrium models of the indicated markets calculated from data provided by the Egyptian Ministries of Agriculture and Supply and the Central Agency for Public Mobilization and Statistics.

Notes: All rows add up to approximately 100, which equals the total burden. Subsidies for inputs other than feed, such as fertilizers and pesticides, are included in the models for specific crops. A negative number indicates a reduction of the burden.

jective, the government had, in principle, all the instruments necessary to reduce the budgeted subsidy expenditures by increasing implicit taxation of the agricultural sector. But the government would not apply them if self-sufficiency were the dominant goal. In that case an increase in explicit food subsidies might be the consequence of efforts to reduce implicit taxation of agriculture in order to increase domestic food output. In this sense there is an inherent conflict between short-term fiscal objectives and self-sufficiency objectives. It is basically the production effects of pricing that determine an optimal long-run solution of this conflict.

A regression model is used here to assess more comprehensively the role of each of the contributors to the total burden. The model evaluates the hypothetical effects on the agricultural burden of the three objectives outlined above: to isolate domestic prices from international price fluctuations, to generate public revenues, and to reduce explicit food subsidies. A quantitative specification for year t is

$$TB_t = f(P_{int,t}, R_t, F_t), \qquad (17)$$

where

TB_t = total burden on agriculture (as defined in equation [16]), multiplied by (-1) in 1975 prices,

$P_{int,t}$ = international price index of agricultural commodities imported to/exported from Egypt (1965/66 average = 1),

R_t = government revenues in 1975 prices, and

F_t = food subsidy expenditure as budgeted in 1975 prices.

The results, in Table 29, show that factors representing the domestic price stabilization objective and the availability of government revenues dominate changes in the burden. The effect of budgeted food subsidies on the change in the total burden is not statistically significant. A 10 percent rise in the index of international agricultural prices increased the burden on agriculture by 13 percent. A 10 percent increase in total government revenues had the opposite effect: it reduced the burden by 16 percent.[115] The impression that explicit food subsidy policies did not increase the burden on agriculture is supported by the model results. The estimation results also reveal how important increased revenues from other sources were in the rapid decrease of the burden. Growing revenues not only reduced the burden induced by price policy but they were also used to support agriculture through public investment (see Chapter 5).

The results do not indicate that agricultural policy is being revised as part of an economic strategy that emphasizes agriculture more and industry less. They simply show a general shift in this direction. The opening of the economy after 1973 affected agriculture only by generating government revenue. However, it is not unlikely that, if government revenues get tight again, agricultural policy will be redirected to increase the burden on agriculture.

The basic findings from the regression model apply not only to commodities as a whole but to basic food commodities as well, as Table 29 shows. Food subsidy expenditures seem to induce higher burdens for these commodities, but again the parameter is hardly statistically significant. Yet it seems possible that the government's actions to reduce the drain from the budget are particularly concentrated on those commodities that induce the food subsidy outlays. But if these actions have any importance at all, it is only a minor effect on agricultural incomes.

The full effects of price, subsidy, and procurement policies do not show up in the official budget as explicit food subsidies. An aggregation of all positive and negative budget effects on the commodity markets shows these effects more completely. In addition to food subsidies, the export taxes for cotton and rice are included here, as well as some of the procurement costs, which were neglected in examining the official subsidy budget. Fiscal costs generated consistently in the welfare analytical framework are used in the aggregation, which is based on the following equation:

---

[115] These implicit elasticities are calculated at mean values from 1965-80 and parameters estimated with equation (17).

74

Table 29—Determinants of changes in the burden on agriculture

Dependent Variable	Independent Variables	R^2	F	D.W.
TB_t =	$1{,}027.0 + 769.8\ P_{int,t} - 0.8404\ R_t + 0.3633\ F_t$ $(3.54)\quad(-7.41)\quad(0.52)$	0.845	21.8	2.21
FB_t =	$468.9 + 582.3\ P_{int,t} - 0.6080\ R_t + 0.6698\ F_t$ $(4.38)\quad(-8.78)\quad(1.58)$	0.899	35.5	2.32
TB_t =	$349.6 + 1{,}011.0\ P_{int,t} - 0.5018\ R_t - 2.236\ A_t$ $(9.16)\quad(-3.64)\quad(-2.81)$	0.904	37.7	2.04
GB_t =	$204.4 + 1{,}043.0\ P_{int,t} - 0.5190\ R_t - 2.452\ A_t$ $(9.16)\quad(-3.64)\quad(-2.81)$	0.912	41.6	2.02

Notes: TB_t is the total burden (implicit taxation) on agriculture in 1975 prices, multiplied by (-1). FB_t is the burden on basic food commodities markets (wheat, rice, maize, pulses, and sugar); GB_t is TB_t with public expenditures on agriculture subtracted; $P_{int,t}$ is the international price index of agricultural commodities imported to or exported from Egypt; R_t is total government revenues in 1975 prices; F_t is food subsidy expenditures as budgeted in 1975 prices; and A_t is net budget spent on agricultural commodities as computed with the partial equilibrium models (sum of government expenditures minus revenues for procured quantities sold on the domestic market, for procured quantities being exported, and for imports sold on domestic markets).

$$A_t = \sum_{i=1}^{8} (B^i_{prc,t} + B^i_{ex,t} + B^i_{im,t}), \qquad (18)$$

where

A_t = the net increase of the budget spent on agricultural commodities,

$B^i_{prc,t}$ = net budget expenditures for procured quantities being sold on the domestic market (net revenues are negative),

$B^i_{ex,t}$ = net budget expenditures for procured quantities being exported (which usually are negative, representing export tax revenues),

$B^i_{im,t}$ = net budget expenditures for imports sold on domestic markets (which are mostly rationed and subsidized commodities, which means this variable also includes explicit food subsidies), and

i = the index for commodities (wheat, rice, maize, beans, lentils, sugar, cotton, and meat).

The explicit food subsidy variable (F) is replaced with this budget effect variable (A) in the equations for TB_t (see Table 29). In equation (19) government outlays for agriculture are combined with agriculture's burden for a more complete picture of the relationship between agriculture and the rest of the economy. It might be argued that parts of the current expenditure budgets of the agricultural ministries have little to do with the agricultural income, as they are mainly for employment in agricultural administration, and may have little effect on production. However, research and extension personnel and those who manage the investment and input provision programs and the water system cannot be separated from those less directly concerned with production. Thus the total agricultural budget, comprising investment (AI) and current expenditures (AC), is deducted from the total burden for the following analysis:[116]

$$GB_t = f(P_{int,t},\ R_t,\ A_t) \qquad (19)$$

---

[116] The input subsidies are already deducted from the burden, so they are not included as exogenous determinants.

where

$$GB_t = TB_t - AI_t - AC_t.$$

Again the results in Table 29 show how important domestic price stabilization is and how revenue affects the burden. Moreover, the higher the government's net expenditures for interventions in the agricultural commodity markets (A_t), the lower the general burden (GB_t). This supports the hypothesis that the burden was reduced as government outlays for food subsidies and agriculture as a whole increased. Self-sufficiency and income support objectives also seem to support this hypothesis. This means that the rising food subsidy bill either had no effect on the burden on agriculture or, perhaps, reduced it.

Conclusions and Policy Implications

Egypt's current food subsidy system did not spring from one decision made in the early 1970s, even though it was then that the huge fiscal outlays which characterize it began. It evolved from existing agricultural and consumer price policies that were implemented a long time before. These policies included export taxes to finance the industrial growth strategy adopted and implicit transfers of income from producers to consumers—implicit food subsidies to finance the cheap food prices. Given this background, it is not surprising that Egypt moved to an explicit food subsidy scheme as the self-sufficiency of major commodities that were implicitly subsidized (such as wheat) decreased rapidly. Indeed, a major change in consumer price policy would have had to occur for Egypt not to have drifted toward an explicit subsidy system in the 1970s, as the time-series analyses for the relevant food commodity markets show.

The course that Egypt's food policies have taken provides an important lesson for countries keeping producer prices low to support consumers. Supply and demand projections show that many of these countries are going to become net importers of food in the years ahead.[117] If they have rather plentiful nonagricultural resources—as Egypt had, mainly because of its rapidly developed oil reserves, the Suez Canal, and foreign assistance—it seems fair to predict that many of these countries are going to drift from implicit to explicit food subsidy schemes, as Egypt did. But when this happens, tight budgets will make severe internal distribution conflicts unavoidable. These countries will have to know more about how to revise their food pricing systems and still ensure nutritional well-being.

Another issue is raised by the conclusion that, in spite of rising budget outlays for food subsidies, the income burden on farm production has been steadily reduced. This reduction was the result of several factors, including changes in procurement policies, adjustments of prices and price ratios, and variations in interventions in agricultural trade. It was particularly a result of rising prices in domestic open food markets. In the course of the 1970s agriculture financed low consumer prices less, and the general taxpayer financed them more. Agriculture's contribution to the system decreased in absolute terms. This means it may not be concluded that consumer subsidies always burden agricultural production. In Egypt, the system's expansion by and large did not. However, it was possible to shift from the implicit to explicit subsidies only because government revenues increased. Foreign assistance had its part in that.

It has been shown that in the early years of exploding food subsidy outlays, public investment in agriculture, already disproportionately low, was reduced further. In recent years more funds have been allocated to promote production of those crops whose output has lagged the most behind demand. This suggests that the countries with cheap food price policies may find themselves under pressure to promote agricultural production. Research forecasting how production and demand develop in specific countries may help those countries to make their policies more timely, so that production can keep up with demand. This could help countries to avoid exploding food subsidy programs, as in Egypt's case.

---

[117] International Food Policy Research Institute, *Food Needs of Developing Countries: Projections of Production and Consumption to 1990,* Research Report 3 (Washington, D.C.: IFPRI, 1977).

It has to be emphasized that the burden on the income of Egypt's farm producers was not reduced primarily by streamlining price distortions in agriculture. Policy changed, partly because of increased subsidies on inputs, so that implicit taxation of basic food commodities was reduced and livestock production was, increasingly, protected. The major inefficiencies in allocation were inherent in Egyptian agricultural policy before the budget outlays for food subsidies began to expand in the 1970s.[118] The net social loss in the production and consumption of all the commodities considered in this study accounted for 1.5 percent of national income in 1979/80. But the increase of the explicit subsidy expenses alone cannot be held responsible for these costs; the total sum of these social costs resulted from distorted prices, as the price policy analysis demonstrated. The bulk of the social costs resulted from the protection of livestock production, the taxation of cotton, and depressed cereal prices, only the latter being partly a result of explicit and implicit food subsidies. As in many other countries, Egypt's agricultural policy has yet to remove distortions in agricultural price ratios and in the terms of trade between agriculture and the rest of the economy, at least insofar as the development strategy does not require that part of the agricultural surplus be taxed indirectly. A removal of price distortions might be needed if agriculture is to grow more rapidly. But, as the analysis of supply response has indicated, it may not be enough. The rigid constraints on resources, deficits of public water and input supply management, and the inefficiency of the agricultural extension service tend to offset the incentives price adjustments give for growth. Price policy should not be viewed as a panacea for Egypt's rural development and national food problems.

Although increasing producer prices while keeping subsidized consumer prices steady might not increase agricultural production significantly, it might still affect rural income growth through multiplier effects that stimulate production and employment in nonagricultural rural sectors.

The expansion of the food subsidy and rationing scheme into rural areas in recent years has increased the transfer of income to both the farm and nonfarm populations in rural areas. Support for producer prices would add to that increase. More microeconomic analyses could improve the understanding of these linkages between sectors and regions and their repercussions on agriculture. Such knowledge might contribute to the design of a comprehensive food policy favoring immediate improvements in nutrition and growth of rural income, as well as easing the adjustments a developing economy needs to make in the longer run.

---

[118] See Hansen and Nashashibi, *Foreign Trade Regimes and Economic Development: Egypt,* for the agricultural price policies in the 1950s and 1960s.

APPENDIX 1:
SUPPLEMENTARY TABLES

Table 30—Net returns of major crops, 1965-80

Year	Wheat	Maize	Rice	Cotton	Long Berseem	Short Berseem
				(LE/feddan)		
1965	8.8	7.9	3.9	29.2	67.6	32.4
1966	16.8	16.0	8.5	9.7	63.4	30.6
1967	9.8	18.3	18.7	25.2	61.0	29.5
1968	4.8	10.0	20.3	35.6	31.3	17.1
1969	3.7	16.0	19.9	48.4	40.0	20.9
1970	19.5	19.9	18.6	27.2	35.4	18.9
1971	18.1	20.0	15.8	30.9	44.8	23.0
1972	18.8	25.2	13.4	46.9	33.8	18.1
1973	32.1	35.3	16.7	34.1	76.9	37.3
1974	45.9	35.6	20.2	42.4	92.3	44.9
1975	43.0	27.9	28.4	31.7	77.8	39.6
1976	26.6	22.2	25.2	60.7	95.9	47.5
1977	50.7	54.2	40.4	44.9	119.5	59.3
1978	74.3	38.6	58.6	82.0	148.0	75.2
1979	58.5	18.7	64.0	123.1	142.7	72.2
1980	28.2	83.0	46.6	107.8	190.0	94.6

Source: Calculated from data provided by the Egyptian Ministry of Agriculture.
Note: The net returns are calculated as yield times price plus the value of by-products minus the cost of production. The cost of production includes labor wages and land rent.

Table 31—Net returns of major rotations, 1965-80

Year	Wheat/Maize	Wheat/Rice	Long Berseem/ Rice	Long Berseem/ Maize	Short Berseem/ Cotton
			(LE/feddan)		
1965	16.7	12.7	71.5	75.5	61.6
1966	32.9	25.4	71.9	79.5	40.3
1967	27.0	27.5	79.8	79.3	54.7
1968	14.8	25.1	51.6	41.3	52.7
1969	19.7	23.6	59.9	56.0	69.4
1970	39.4	38.1	54.0	55.3	46.2
1971	38.0	33.8	60.5	64.7	53.8
1972	44.0	32.3	47.3	59.0	65.0
1973	67.4	48.8	93.6	112.2	71.4
1974	81.5	66.1	112.5	127.9	87.3
1975	71.0	71.4	106.1	105.7	71.3
1976	48.8	51.8	121.1	118.1	108.2
1977	104.9	91.1	159.9	173.8	104.2
1978	113.0	132.9	206.7	186.7	157.2
1979	77.1	122.5	206.7	161.4	195.3
1980	111.2	74.8	236.5	273.1	202.4

Source: Calculated from data provided by the Egyptian Ministry of Agriculture.
Note: The net returns are calculated as yield times price plus the value of by-products minus the cost of production. The cost of production includes labor wages and land rent.

Table 32—Calculation of border prices at farm gate for wheat, 1965-80

Year	Import Unit Value	Marketing Cost	Foreign Exchange Bias	Border Price
		(LE/metric ton)		
1965	32.0	3.6	33.7	69.3
1966	30.0	4.2	33.3	67.5
1967	31.0	4.2	30.5	65.7
1968	27.0	4.2	24.8	56.0
1969	27.0	4.2	29.5	60.7
1970	29.9	4.2	33.2	67.3
1971	27.7	4.8	25.4	57.8
1972	28.3	4.8	24.2	57.3
1973	63.2	4.8	46.1	114.1
1974	88.5	5.4	55.8	149.7
1975	73.1	6.0	59.6	138.7
1976	60.1	6.6	53.8	120.6
1977	47.2	7.2	39.7	94.1
1978	52.4	8.4	44.1	104.9
1979	125.3	9.0	9.4	143.7
1980	149.7	11.4	25.8	186.9

Sources: The import unit values for 1965-69 are from the Central Agency for Public Mobilization and Statistics and the values for 1970-80 are from the Egyptian Ministry of Supply. The marketing costs are from Black and Vetch International, "Master Plan for the Development of Egyptian Storage and Distribution System for Food Grains," paper prepared for the General Authority for Supply Commodities, Cairo, 1978.

Notes: The foreign exchange bias was calculated from the official and shadow exchange rates (see Table 6). The border price is the sum of the import unit values, marketing costs, and foreign exchange bias.

Table 33—Calculation of border prices at farm gate for rice, 1965-80

Year	Export Unit Value	Marketing Cost	Processing and Milling	Foreign Exchange Bias	Border Price
			(LE/metric ton)		
1965	62.3	7.5	2.6	65.6	123.0
1966	65.2	8.2	2.6	72.4	132.0
1967	69.6	8.2	2.0	68.4	131.8
1968	81.4	8.1	2.0	74.6	149.9
1969	73.1	8.4	2.2	79.7	146.6
1970	53.0	8.7	2.1	58.8	105.2
1971	49.5	9.0	2.1	45.4	88.0
1972	50.1	9.1	2.0	42.8	85.8
1973	90.7	9.5	2.0	66.2	149.4
1974	291.4	10.6	3.1	183.7	467.7
1975	238.4	11.6	3.2	194.4	424.4
1976	154.0	12.8	4.1	138.0	283.3
1977	108.2	14.4	4.2	91.1	189.0
1978	136.7	16.0	3.8	115.0	239.6
1979	232.4	17.6	4.7	17.5	237.0
1980	251.2	21.6	9.4	43.2	282.3

Sources: The export unit values for 1965-69 are from the Central Agency for Public Mobilization and Statistics and the values for 1970-80 are from the Egyptian Ministry of Supply. The marketing costs are from Black and Vetch International, "Master Plan for the Development of Egyptian Storage and Distribution System for Food Grains," paper prepared for the General Authority for Supply Commodities, Cairo, 1978.

Notes: The foreign exchange bias was calculated from the official and shadow exchange rates (see Table 6). The border price is the sum of the export unit values, marketing and processing costs, and foreign exchange bias.

Table 34—Calculation of border prices at farm gate for beef, 1965-80

Year	Import Unit Value	Marketing Cost	Foreign Exchange Bias	Border Price
		(LE/metric ton)		
1965	329	19.9	346.6	695.5
1966	282	21.7	313.0	616.7
1967	251	21.9	246.7	519.6
1968	198	21.6	181.5	401.1
1969	216	22.3	235.6	473.9
1970	233	23.1	258.7	514.8
1971	309	23.8	283.3	616.1
1972	242	24.3	206.9	473.2
1973	465	25.4	339.3	829.7
1974	416	28.1	262.3	706.4
1975	300	30.9	244.7	575.6
1976	323	34.0	289.5	646.5
1977	471	38.3	396.5	905.8
1978	436	42.6	367.0	845.6
1979	1,173	46.9	88.2	1,308.1
1980	1,128	57.5	194.2	1,379.7

Sources: The import unit values for 1965-69 are from the Central Agency for Public Mobilization and Statistics and the values for 1970-80 are from the Egyptian Ministry of Supply. The marketing costs are from Ibrahim Soliman, "Red Meat Price Policy in Egypt," Economics Working Paper 62, Agricultural Development Systems Project, Ministry of Agriculture, Cairo, and the University of California-Berkeley, Cairo, 1982.

Notes: The foreign exchange bias was calculated from the official and shadow exchange rates (see Table 6). The border price is the sum of the import unit values, marketing costs, and foreign exchange bias.

APPENDIX 2:

THE CALCULATIONS OF THE EFFECTS OF GOVERNMENT INTERVENTION IN SELECTED MARKETS

The effects of government intervention in the wheat, rice, red meat, and feed markets were discussed in Chapter 6. The calculations of those effects are described here.

The price elasticities of demand used are, for wheat, -0.13; for rice, -0.01; for maize, -0.13; for beans and lentils, -0.38; for sugar, -0.40; for red meat, -0.72; for milk, -0.84; and for cotton, -0.20. The wheat price elasticity is a weighted average of estimated coefficients for wheat grain, bread, and flour. The elasticity for cotton is not based on an estimation result; it is an informed guess. All were calculated from disaggregated results in the annex to Joachim von Braun, "A Demand System for Egypt."

The abbreviations used in this appendix follow:

B_{ex} = increase in the government's budget because of exports;

B_{im} = increase in the government's budget because of imports;

B_{prc} = increase in the government's budget because of procurement and distribution;

B_{tot} = total increase in the government's budget;

G_{dis}^c = income transfer from or to consumers by government distribution.

G_{fre}^c = income transfer from or to consumers in the open market;

G_{fre}^p = income transfer from or to producers in the open market;

G_{prc}^p = income transfer from or to producers from procurement;

G_{soc}^c = net social loss in consumption;

G_{soc}^p = net social loss in production;

G_{tot}^c = total consumer loss or gain;

G_{tot}^p = total producer loss or gain;

K_1 = milling and handling costs for feed mix production;

m = marketing and handling costs per unit;

P_{dis}^c = the price for quantities distributed by the government (subsidized or rationed);

P_{dis2}^c = second tier subsidized/rationed price (or urban free price);

P_{dis}^p = the domestic price paid by the farmer;

P_{fre}^c = the free market consumer price;

P_{fre}^p = the free market producer price (at the farm gate);

P_{int} = the border price equivalent at the shadow exchange rate;

P_{int}^o = the border price equivalent at the official exchange rate;

P_{prc}^p = the procurement price;

Q_{dem} = the quantity consumed domestically (production, trade, waste, industrial use, change in stocks, animal feed, with seed for the crop subtracted);

Q_{dis} = the quantity distributed by the government (rationed and subsidized);

$Q_{fe,i}$ = the quantity of feed of commodity i;

Q_{fre} = the quantity marketed on the open market;

Q_{hum} = human consumption of maize and sorghum estimated from family budget surveys, and consumption projected to 1980 from the per capita trend of 1964/65-1974/75;

Q_{im} = the quantity imported (net imports);

$Q_{im,fe}$ = the quantity of feed imported;

Q_{ind} = the quantity used by industry;

Q_{prc} = the quantity procured from domestic production;

Q_{prd} = the quantity produced domestically;

Q_{sc} = the change in stocks;

Q_{se} = the quantity used as seeds;

$Q_{st,c}$, $Q_{st,r}$ = the quantity of starch units in concentrates (c) or roughage (r);

Q_w = the quantity wasted;

S = input subsidies per unit;

t_{fre}^{p} = the tax rate on the producer price;

t_{fre}^{c} = the tax rate on the consumer price;

η_s = the price elasticity of supply (for the definition, see Chapter 6); and

η_d = the price elasticity of demand.

Wheat, Rice, and Red Meat Markets

The calculations of the effects of government intervention in the wheat market are based on the following set of equations:

Producer loss or gain from procurement:

$$G_{prc}^{p} = Q_{prc} \cdot (P_{prc}^{p} + S - P_{int}).$$

Producer loss or gain in free market sales:

$$G_{fre}^{p} = (Q_{prd} - Q_{prc}) \cdot (P_{fre}^{p} + S - P_{int}).$$

Net social loss in production:

$$G_{soc}^{p} = \tfrac{1}{2} \cdot (t_{fre}^{p})^{2} \cdot \eta_s \cdot Q_{prd} \cdot P_{fre}^{p}.$$

The producer loss or gain:

$$G_{tot}^{p} = G_{prc}^{p} + G_{fre}^{p} - G_{soc}^{p}.$$

Consumer loss or gain from government wheat distribution:

$$Q_{dem} = Q_{prd} + Q_{im} - Q_{ind} - Q_{se} - Q_{w} - Q_{sc},$$

and

$$G_{dis}^{c} = (Q_{dem} - Q_{prd} + Q_{prc}) \cdot (P_{int} - P_{fre}^{c}).$$

Consumer loss or gain in free market purchases:

$$G_{fre}^{c} = (Q_{prd} - Q_{prc}) \cdot (P_{int} - P_{fre}^{c}).$$

Net social loss in consumption:

$$G_{soc}^{c} = \tfrac{1}{2} (t_{fre}^{c})^{2} \cdot \eta_d \cdot Q_{dem} \cdot P_{fre}^{c}.$$

Total consumer loss or gain:

$$G_{tot}^{c} = G_{dis}^{c} + G_{fre}^{c} - G_{soc}^{c}.$$

Increase in government's budget from procurement and distribution:

$$B_{prc} = Q_{prc} \cdot (P_{prc}^{p} + m - P_{dis}^{c}).$$

Increase in government's budget from the subsidized distribution of imports (calculated at the official exchange rate):

$$B_{im} = Q_{im} \cdot (P_{int}^{o} + m - P_{dis}^{c}).$$

Total budget increase:

$$B_{tot} = B_{prc} + B_{im}.$$

The calculations of the effects of government intervention in the rice and red meat markets follow the same logic as those for wheat. The other markets discussed in Chapter 6, maize, pulses, sugar, cotton, and milk, are similarly modeled. The details and computation results of the model are available from the authors. They are adjusted for exports, milling, and other utilization ratios for the commodity. For some commodities, G_{prc}^{p} or G_{dis}^{c} is zero. The results for these markets are given in Tables 35-37.

Feed Market Analysis

The analysis of the feed market has four parts. The first, the data used to determine the demand for feed, is given in Table 38. The second, the total feed requirement, is given in Table 39. The other two parts are the calculations of the supply of feed and of feed subsidies.

Calculation of Feed Supply

The supply of the by-products of milling and processing, wheat bran, rice bran, and cottonseed cake, is given by:

$$Q_{fe,i} = e_i \cdot (Q_{prd,i} + Q_{im,i} - Q_{ind,i\neq2,3} - Q_{se,i} - Q_{sc,i}) + Q_{im,fe},$$

Table 35—Model computations for the wheat market, 1965-80

Year	Q_{prd}	Q_{im}	Q_{prc}	Q_{dem}	Q_{dis}	Q_{fre}
			(1,000 metric tons)			
1965	1,271.6	2,326.0	229.0	3,293.6	2,251.0	1,042.6
1966	1,465.9	2,127.0	258.0	2,916.9	1,709.0	1,207.9
1967	1,290.5	2,817.0	249.0	3,349.5	2,308.0	1,041.5
1968	1,517.6	2,269.0	283.0	3,158.6	1,924.0	1,234.6
1969	1,269.0	2,706.0	134.6	4,331.0	3,196.6	1,134.4
1970	1,517.1	2,568.0	182.1	4,555.1	3,220.1	1,335.0
1971	1,730.1	2,782.0	285.6	3,679.1	2,234.6	1,444.5
1972	1,615.1	2,682.0	241.1	4,222.1	2,848.1	1,374.0
1973	1,838.3	3,171.5	282.4	4,683.8	3,127.9	1,555.9
1974	1,884.5	3,547.8	359.4	4,815.3	3,290.2	1,525.1
1975	2,032.5	3,914.0	381.6	4,600.5	2,949.6	1,650.9
1976	1,960.0	3,709.5	301.2	5,070.5	3,411.7	1,658.8
1977	1,697.3	4,453.1	138.5	5,513.4	3,954.6	1,558.8
1978	1,933.0	5,564.0	127.5	6,843.0	5,037.5	1,805.5
1979	1,856.0	4,905.6	289.3	6,601.6	5,034.9	1,566.7
1980	1,796.0	5,599.6	125.2	6,898.6	5,227.8	1,670.8

Year	G_{prc}^{p}	G_{fre}^{p}	G_{soc}^{p}	G_{tot}^{p}	G_{dis}^{c}	G_{fre}^{c}
			(LE million)			
1965	−10.1	−37.3	−10.0	−37.5	89.6	34.7
1966	−10.2	−33.0	−9.1	−34.2	64.9	28.8
1967	−9.6	−19.0	4.7	−33.3	82.1	13.9
1968	−8.6	−8.7	0.8	−18.1	45.2	2.2
1969	−4.7	−26.8	−7.5	−24.0	90.1	20.6
1970	−6.7	−35.9	−10.0	−32.5	112.1	28.2
1971	−7.9	−29.4	−8.8	−28.5	56.8	22.1
1972	−6.2	−26.7	−7.4	−25.5	70.7	21.4
1973	−22.8	−104.2	−26.6	−100.4	249.8	99.9
1974	−36.5	−133.1	−33.5	−136.1	346.9	135.7
1975	−31.2	−115.5	−27.4	−119.3	278.6	123.4
1976	−19.4	−94.5	−20.9	−93.1	260.3	103.8
1977	−4.9	−35.3	−5.9	−34.2	197.1	43.8
1978	−5.6	−26.7	2.9	−35.1	293.5	35.4
1979	−19.9	−100.8	−22.4	−98.4	488.8	109.9
1980	−12.5	−153.9	−32.3	−134.1	699.1	162.0

Year	G_{soc}^{c}	G_{tot}^{c}	B_{prc}	B_{im}	B_{tot}
			(LE million)		
1965	6.6	117.7	−0.4	14.1	13.7
1966	2.5	91.2	0.5	10.0	10.4
1967	0.7	95.2	0.1	14.3	14.4
1968	0.0	47.3	−1.0	−2.9	−3.9
1969	2.2	108.5	−0.4	−3.4	−3.9
1970	2.9	137.4	0.2	4.2	4.4
1971	1.3	77.6	0.4	0.1	0.5
1972	1.6	90.5	0.7	1.7	2.4
1973	25.2	324.6	0.9	107.1	107.9
1974	40.8	441.8	2.9	176.0	178.9
1975	26.1	375.8	6.7	136.3	143.0
1976	22.2	341.8	5.1	83.2	88.3
1977	4.3	238.7	2.8	45.1	47.9
1978	2.0	328.9	2.7	72.8	81.5
1979	28.7	570.0	10.2	430.0	440.3
1980	46.9	814.2	5.4	604.6	610.0

Table 36—Model computations for the rice market, 1965-80

Year	Q_{prd}	Q_{ex}	Q_{prc}	Q_{dem}	Q_{dis}	Q_{fre}
			(1,000 metric tons)			
1965	1,786.9	311	894	848.3	254.8	593.5
1966	1,674.9	311	839	877.4	220.0	657.4
1967	2,275.5	419	1,156	871.9	312.6	559.2
1968	2,582.7	555	1,322	920.5	281.7	638.8
1969	2,557.0	762	1,342	899.9	87.4	812.5
1970	2,603.0	646	1,154	952.9	84.4	868.5
1971	2,535.7	480	1,068	1,045.9	195.9	849.9
1972	2,512.4	433	1,021	1,078.5	213.2	865.3
1973	2,270.6	293	925	1,074.2	292.4	781.8
1974	2,238.9	136	866	1,185.8	412.1	773.7
1975	2,427.9	102	1,166	1,247.7	636.0	611.7
1976	2,300.0	208	1,086	1,255.5	479.3	776.1
1977	2,272.0	221	1,054	1,142.7	446.1	696.6
1978	2,351.0	146	1,107	1,266.5	554.6	711.8
1979	2,511.0	175	1,305	1,336.2	651.0	685.3
1980	2,384.0	100	1,222	1,332.8	673.5	659.4

Year	G^p_{prc}	G^p_{fre}	G^p_{soc}	G^p_{tot}	G^c_{dis}	G^c_{fre}
			(LE million)			
1965	−52.0	−44.6	14.0	−110.5	23.8	47.2
1966	−53.9	−37.8	11.9	−103.6	20.5	47.1
1967	−66.3	−46.5	15.0	−127.9	18.3	36.6
1968	−91.2	−59.1	19.3	−169.6	27.3	46.9
1969	−90.2	−69.3	23.2	−182.7	13.3	72.5
1970	−47.4	−48.6	14.2	−110.3	6.4	45.1
1971	−32.1	−34.1	9.8	−76.0	8.2	30.4
1972	−28.8	−33.7	9.2	−71.7	9.1	30.9
1973	−62.6	−80.3	21.1	−164.0	32.6	74.6
1974	−226.4	−347.2	87.2	−660.7	171.0	313.4
1975	−261.7	−277.9	81.6	−621.1	238.0	217.8
1976	−135.4	−148.6	42.2	−326.1	111.4	157.1
1977	−68.4	−69.6	18.7	−156.7	61.2	69.4
1978	−90.7	−96.3	26.7	−213.6	96.5	93.7
1979	−105.2	−86.6	26.4	−218.3	92.3	84.0
1980	−121.4	−106.3	32.4	−260.1	120.6	101.6

Year	G^c_{soc}	G^c_{tot}	B_{prc}	B_{ex}	B_{tot}
			(LE million)		
1965	0.6	70.5	−1.4	8.0	−9.4
1966	0.3	67.2	−4.5	8.7	−13.2
1967	0.2	54.7	−10.7	8.7	−19.4
1968	0.3	73.9	−7.5	18.1	−25.6
1969	0.6	85.3	−1.0	18.5	−19.4
1970	0.2	51.3	−0.7	2.4	−3.2
1971	0.1	38.5	−1.5	0.0	−1.5
1972	0.1	39.9	−0.9	0.1	−1.1
1973	0.8	106.3	−1.2	11.9	−13.0
1974	14.5	469.9	1.6	31.7	−30.1
1975	10.8	445.0	13.3	17.0	−3.7
1976	2.9	265.5	14.2	13.8	0.4
1977	0.5	130.0	12.8	4.2	8.7
1978	0.9	189.3	24.7	3.2	21.5
1979	0.8	175.5	11.9	20.4	−8.5
1980	1.0	221.2	15.6	12.0	3.5

Sources and notes for Tables 35 and 36

Sources: Calculated from data provided by the Egyptian Ministries of Agriculture and Supply and the Principal Bank for Development and Agricultural Investment.

Notes: Q_{prd} is the quantity of paddy produced domestically; Q_{im}, the quantity imported; Q_{ex}, the quantity exported; Q_{prc}, the quantity procured from domestic production; Q_{dem}, the quantity consumed domestically; Q_{dis}, the quantity distributed by the government; and Q_{fre}, the quantity marketed on the open market. G_{prc}^p is the income transfer from or to producers from procurement; G_{fre}^p, the income transfer from or to producers in the open market; G_{soc}^p, the net social loss in production; and G_{tot}^p, the total producer loss or gain. G_{dis}^c is the income transfer from or to consumers by government distribution; G_{fre}^c, the income transfer from or to consumers in the open market; G_{soc}^c, the net social loss in consumption; and G_{tot}^c, the total consumer loss or gain. B_{prc} is the increase in the government's budget because of procurement and distribution; B_{im}, the increase in the budget because of imports; B_{ex}, the increase in the budget because of exports; and B_{tot}, the total increase in the budget.

Table 37—Model computations for the beef market, 1965-80

Year	Q_{prd}	Q_{dem}	Q_{im}	G_{fre}^p	G_{soc}^p	G_{tot}^p
	(1,000 metric tons)			(LE million)		
1965	241	296	55	−97.2	8.2	−105.3
1966	284	338	54	−88.4	19.0	−107.4
1967	332	359	27	−69.0	5.3	−74.4
1968	348	371	23	−27.5	0.5	−28.0
1969	340	363	23	−42.2	1.3	−43.5
1970	295	330	35	−41.5	1.4	−42.9
1971	282	321	39	−67.8	5.2	−73.0
1972	291	325	34	−23.5	0.4	−23.8
1973	313	354	41	−123.0	22.6	−145.6
1974	326	396	70	−72.0	3.3	−75.4
1975	337	386	49	19.0	0.1	18.9
1976	302	400	98	34.8	0.3	34.5
1977	323	394	71	−12.7	0.0	−12.8
1978	337	447	110	28.2	0.2	28.0
1979	326	408	82	−90.6	2.3	−92.9
1980	336	448	112	41.7	0.2	41.5

Year	G_{fre}^c	G_{dis}^c	G_{soc}^c	G_{tot}^c	B_{im}
	(LE million)				
1965	68.2	12.2	20.7	59.7	−6.9
1966	48.6	3.4	8.0	44.0	−13.5
1967	25.1	−1.1	1.7	22.4	−7.8
1968	−2.5	−3.8	0.0	−6.3	−8.0
1969	17.6	−1.2	0.8	15.6	−6.6
1970	0.7	−4.4	0.0	−3.7	−13.5
1971	16.7	−3.3	0.7	12.6	−14.4
1972	−33.0	−9.8	2.6	−45.4	−16.8
1973	59.0	0.8	7.1	52.7	−13.1
1974	−0.6	1.8	0.0	1.3	−16.5
1975	−88.5	−5.1	11.4	−105.1	−17.1
1976	−145.7	−3.3	29.7	−178.7	−31.7
1977	−104.1	16.0	12.0	−100.1	−12.1
1978	−135.7	18.2	20.9	−138.4	−22.2
1979	−7.3	51.5	0.1	44.1	44.3
1980	−171.6	78.4	22.3	−115.5	56.6

Sources: Calculated from data provided by the Egyptian Ministries of Agriculture and Supply and the Principal Bank for Development and Agricultural Investment.

Notes: Q_{prd} is the quantity produced domestically; Q_{dem}, the quantity consumed domestically; and Q_{im}, the quantity imported (net imports). G_{fre}^p is the income transfer from or to producers in the open market; G_{soc}^p, the net social loss in production; and G_{tot}^p, the total producer loss or gain. G_{fre}^c is the income transfer from or to consumers in the open market; G_{dis}^c, the income transfer from or to consumers by government distribution; G_{soc}^c, the net social loss in consumption; and G_{tot}^c, the total consumer loss or gain. B_{im} is the increase in the government's budget because of imports distributed at the subsidized price.

Table 38—Energy demand per unit of livestock and livestock numbers, selected years

Type of Livestock/Age	Energy Demand	Share of Total Stock	Livestock			
			Total Stock			
			1965	1970	1975	1980
	(1,000 starch units/year/head)	(percent)	(1,000 head)			
Cattle	0.9075	100.0	1,608	2,115	2,102	2,120
Over 2 years	1.1	51.6				
1 – 2 years	0.84	28.2				
Less than 1 year	0.51	20.2				
Buffalo	1.277	100.0	1,617	2,009	2,204	2,379
Over 2 years	1.544	63.7				
1 – 2 years	0.95	20.7				
Less than 1 year	0.62	15.6				
Sheep and goats	0.243	100.0	2,642	3,221	3,247	4,189
Horses	1.46	100.0	56	35	29	30
Camels	2.19	100.0	175	127	105	100
Donkeys	0.73	100.0	1,138	1,392	1,533	1,500
			(1,000 metric tons)			
Poultry	2.5[a]	100.0	86	96	110	123
Eggs	3.5[a]	100.0	40	50	60	77

Sources: Data on energy demands of livestock are taken from Alois Grosse-Rueschkamp, "Optimal Planning of Feed Mix Industries in Egypt" (Ph.D. thesis, University of Bonn, 1979). (In German.) The age distribution of livestock is taken from James B. Fitch and Ibrahim Soliman, "The Livestock Economy in Egypt: An Appraisal of the Current Situation," Cairo, 1982 (mimeographed). The data on total stock comes from Egypt, Central Agency for Public Mobilization and Statistics.

[a] This figure is in 1,000 starch units per year per metric ton.

Table 39—Total requirements of feed, 1965-80

Year	Poultry and Eggs		Cattle and Buffalo		Other Livestock		Total
	Require-ments	Share of Total	Require-ments	Share of Total	Require-ments	Share of Total	Require-ments
	(1,000 metric tons of starch units)	(percent)	(1,000 metric tons of starch units)	(percent)	(1,000 metric tons of starch units)	(percent)	(1,000 metric tons of starch units)
1965	355.0	6.1	3,524.0	60.5	1,937.7	33.3	5,816.7
1966	382.5	6.4	3,581.0	60.2	1,982.2	33.3	5,945.7
1967	410.0	6.7	3,637.0	59.8	2,028.4	33.3	6,075.5
1968	410.5	6.0	4,348.6	64.5	1,978.7	29.3	6,737.8
1969	399.5	5.8	4,417.1	64.2	2,061.2	29.9	6,877.8
1970	415.0	5.9	4,484.6	63.8	2,128.0	30.2	7,027.7
1971	430.5	6.1	4,544.5	64.4	2,081.1	29.4	7,056.1
1972	450.0	6.2	4,611.0	64.0	2,140.2	29.7	7,201.2
1973	458.0	6.3	4,656.4	64.1	2,148.7	29.5	7,263.1
1974	471.0	6.4	4,693.8	64.0	2,158.2	29.4	7,323.1
1975	485.0	6.5	4,721.8	63.9	2,180.4	29.5	7,387.2
1976	508.0	6.8	4,741.8	63.8	2,181.3	29.3	7,431.2
1977	547.5	7.3	4,752.0	63.4	2,186.2	29.2	7,485.7
1978	543.0	7.0	4,820.1	62.6	2,328.3	30.2	7,691.4
1979	561.0	7.1	4,890.4	62.6	2,351.6	30.1	7,803.1
1980	577.0	7.2	4,961.6	62.6	2,375.7	30.0	7,914.3

Sources: Calculated from data provided by the Egyptian Ministry of Agriculture. The amounts required per head were taken from Alois Grosse-Rueschkamp, "Optimal Planning of Feed Mix Industries in Egypt" (Ph.D. thesis, University of Bonn, 1979). (In German.)

Note: The calculated total requirements deviate from the total supply calculated in Table 40 because of differences in the estimation procedures for supply and requirements.

where i equals 1, wheat bran; 2, rice bran; or 3, cottonseed cake; and e_i equals the extraction rates of the by-products. The extraction rate for wheat—the wheat milling rate—as calculated from data provided by the Ministry of Supply and Home Trade, was 0.83 in 1965, 0.90 in 1966, 0.92 in 1967 and 1968, 0.88 from 1969 to 1972, 0.82 in 1973 and 1974, and 0.87 from 1975 to 1980. The rice bran extraction rate was 0.062, and the cottonseed cake extraction rate was 0.44 percent. Raw paddy contains 14 percent husk; the rest yields 9 percent bran, 80 percent of which is used for feed and 20 percent of which is processed into bran oil. Raw cotton contains 64 percent seed, of which 69 percent is processed into cottonseed cake.

The supply of maize, sorghum, and barley for feed is calculated by:

$$Q_{fe,i} = Q_{prd,i} + Q_{im,i} - Q_{ind,i}$$
$$- Q_{w,i} - Q_{se,i} - Q_{sc,i} - Q_{hum,i},$$

where i equals 4, maize; 5, sorghum; or 6, barley.

Human consumption is estimated using data in family budget surveys for rural and urban per capita consumption ($c_{r,i}$ and $c_{u,i}$), multiplied by population (POP_r or POP_u). The consumption figures between the family budget surveys (1964/65 and 1974/75) are interpolated, and the figures are extrapolated to 1980:

$$c_{i,t} = POP_{r,t} \cdot c_{r,i,t} + POP_{u,t} \cdot c_{u,i,t},$$

where t equals 1965, . . . , 1980 and i equals 4 (maize) or 5 (sorghum). The figures for the human consumption of barley were taken from Food and Agriculture Organization of the United Nations, *Food Balance Sheets 1965-80* (Rome: FAO, 1982).

The supply of berseem is given by:

$$Q_{fe,i} = \sum_{j=1}^{3} yield_j \cdot area_j,$$

where i equals 7, berseem, and where $yield_j$ is the yield of long season berseem (j equals 1, 22 tons per feddan), short season berseem (j equals 2, 9.7 tons per feddan), and seed berseem (j equals 3, 19.5 tons per feddan), and where $area_j$ is the area of these same three types of berseem.

Similarly, the supply of straw is given by:

$$Q_{fe,i} = \sum_{j=1}^{4} straw_j \cdot area_j,$$

where i equals 8, straw, and where $straw_j$ is is the yield of straw from wheat (j equals 1, 1.68 tons per feddan), barley (j equals 2, 1.22 tons per feddan), beans (j equals 3, 1.1 tons per feddan), and lentils (j equals 4, 0.76 tons per feddan), and where $area_j$ is the area of these same four sources of straw.

Green fodder of maize is a by-product of maize production obtained by stripping the stalks of their green leaves. The yield is assumed to be 0.43 tons per feddan of maize, so the supply of green maize leaves is given by:

$$Q_{fe,i} = 0.43 \cdot area_i,$$

where i equals 9, green maize leaves.

These components of total feed supplies are aggregated using the units of starch they contain as weights. The total starch units in concentrates are given by:

$$Q_{st,c} = 0.49 \cdot Q_{fe,1} + 0.23 \cdot Q_{fe,2}$$
$$+ 0.43 \cdot Q_{fe,3} + 0.81 \cdot Q_{im,4} + 0.74$$
$$\cdot (Q_{fe,4} - Q_{im,4}) + 0.6 \cdot Q_{fe,5}$$
$$+ 0.72 \cdot Q_{fe,6}.$$

The total starch units in green fodder roughage are given by:

$$Q_{st,r} = 0.08 \cdot Q_{fe,7} + 0.145$$
$$\cdot Q_{fe,8} + 0.1 \cdot Q_{fe,9},$$

and the total supply of starch units is given by:

$$Q_{st} = Q_{st,c} + Q_{st,r}.$$

The results of the calculations of the feed supply are given in Table 40.

Calculation of Feed Subsidies

The subsidy on feed mix is given by:

$$S_i = Q_{dis,i} (P_{int,i} - P^p_{dis,i}),$$

where i equals 1, feed mix. The data for $Q_{dis,i}$ come from the Principal Bank for Develop-

Table 40—Feed supply, 1965-80

| | Major Feed Components | | | | | | Total Supply | | |
Year	Wheat Bran	Rice Bran	Maize	Sorghum and Barley	Cotton-seed Cake	Berseem	Concen-trates	Fodder and Roughage	Total
	(1,000 metric tons)						(1,000 starch units)		
1965	406.9	113.9	787.5	311.3	630.3	41,975.6	1,162.9	3,745.3	4,908.1
1966	224.0	116.8	978.5	378.6	540.1	43.352.0	1,159.3	3,885.3	5,044.7
1967	197.6	126.9	947.0	421.5	525.1	47,674.1	1,110.3	4,204.1	5,314.8
1968	194.3	145.0	1,039.0	510.2	528.9	48,719.8	1,198.2	4,330.4	5,528.6
1969	385.9	163.3	1,073.6	496.4	651.3	49,581.7	1,353.4	4,360.1	5,713.5
1970	428.8	157.1	1,167.1	543.2	605.5	49,052.2	1,420.6	4,323.0	5,743.6
1971	285.3	150.0	1,067.3	580.5	619.2	50,975.1	1,275.3	4,481.0	5,756.3
1972	417.0	148.6	1,216.2	556.2	617.6	51,665.7	1,470.2	4,525.4	5,995.6
1973	727.3	134.4	1,293.4	559.6	575.8	50,766.3	1,651.2	4,445.7	6,096.9
1974	719.4	129.9	1,587.6	540.3	522.2	51,266.5	1,858.3	4,509.9	6,368.1
1975	484.8	132.7	1,777.8	548.3	437.5	52,139.7	1,867.0	4,589.8	6,456.8
1976	558.6	143.8	2,191.6	559.0	448.7	52,232.0	2,223.1	4,601.7	6,824.8
1977	596.9	134.0	2,118.1	489.1	499.4	53,559.3	2,808.2	4,662.6	6,870.8
1978	702.6	138.8	2,807.9	558.9	527.2	53,699.1	2,808.2	4,710.7	7,518.9
1979	681.5	148.5	2,390.3	526.7	532.6	53,298.7	2,474.0	4,678.8	7,152.8
1980	734.5	140.8	2,947.8	555.2	615.7	52,265.1	2,978.8	4,581.6	7,560.4

Sources: These are calculated from data provided by the Egyptian Ministries of Agriculture and Supply and the Central Agency for Public Mobilization and Statistics.

Note: The calculated total supply deviates from the total requirements calculated in Table 39 because of differences in the estimation procedures for supply and requirements.

ment and Agricultural Investment. In calculating $P_{int,i}$, the average composition of all feed mix was assumed to equal the composition for cattle. $P_{int,i}$ was calculated using the formula

$$P_{int,1} = \sum_{j=1}^{6} \alpha_j P_{int,j} + K_1,$$

where j equals 1, cottonseed cake; 2, wheat bran; 3, rice bran; 4, maize; 5, molasses; and 6, minerals; and where α_j is the time variant share of feed component j in the total feed mix. The shares for 1965 and 1980 are listed below as examples:

	1965	1980
α_1	0.55	0.28
α_2	0.30	0.30
α_3	0.10	0.04
α_4	0.00	0.32
α_5	0.02	0.03
α_6	0.03	0.03

The subsidies of the individual components of concentrates not included in the feed mix were calculated using this equation:

$$S_i = (Q_{fe,j} - \alpha_i \cdot Q_{dis,1}) \cdot (P_{int,i} - P^p_{dis,i}),$$

where i equals 2, cottonseed cake; 3, wheat bran; 4, rice bran; and 5, maize; and j equals 1, cottonseed cake; 2, wheat bran; 3, rice bran; and 4, maize. It is assumed that the price of minerals and molasses are free from distortion.

The subsidy of berseem is given by:

$$S_i = Q_{fe,i} \cdot (P_{int,7} - P^p_{fre,7}),$$

where i equals 6. The international equivalent price of berseem, $P_{int,7}$, is derived from the international equivalent price of feed mix ($P_{int,1}$) and the domestic price of straw (P_{straw}), using the following relationship:[119]

$$P_{int,7} = (P_{int,1} + P_{straw}) \cdot 0.10.$$

---

[119] Ingram and Moursi, "Treating Berseem as a Traded Good."

Bibliography

Abdel-Khalek, Gouda and Tignor, Robert L., eds. *The Political Economy of Income Distribution in Egypt.* New York: Holmes and Meier, 1981.

Abdel-Fadil, Mahmoud. *Development, Income Distribution and Social Change in Rural Egypt (1952-1970).* Department of Applied Economics, Occasional Paper No. 45. Cambridge: Cambridge University Press, 1975.

Adams, Richard. "Growth Without Development in Rural Egypt: A Local-level Study of Institutional and Social Change." Ph.D. thesis, University of California, Berkeley, 1981.

Alderman, Harold; von Braun, Joachim; and Sakr, Sakr Ahmed. *Egypt's Food Subsidy and Rationing System: A Description.* Research Report 34. Washington, D.C.: International Food Policy Research Institute, 1982.

Askari, Hossein and Cummings, John T. *Agricultural Supply Response, A Survey of the Econometric Evidence.* New York: Praeger Publishers, 1976.

Atkinson, Anthony B. and Stiglitz, Joseph E. *Lectures on Public Economics.* New York: McGraw-Hill Book Co., 1980.

Badawy, Ismail. Deputy Minister of Economy, Egypt. Personal communications, 1981-82.

Bale, Malcom D. and Lutz, Ernst. "Price Distortions in Agriculture and their Effects: An International Comparison." *American Journal of Agricultural Economics* 63 (January 1981): 8-22.

Barghout, Saad. Undersecretary, Ministry of Economy, Ministry of Planning, Egypt. Personal communications, 1981-82.

Baumgarten, Klaus. "Zuckerwirtschaft in Ägypten" [Sugar Economy in Egypt]. *Zuckerindustrie* 104 (September 1979): 854-859.

Black and Vetch International. "Master Plan for the Development of Egyptian Storage and Distribution System for Food Grains." Paper prepared for General Authority for Supply Commodities, Cairo, 1978.

Braun, Joachim von. "Agricultural Sector Analysis and Food Supply in Egypt." Interim Report of the Joint Project of the Institute of Agricultural Economics, University of Göttingen, and the Institute of National Planning, Cairo, February 1980 (mimeographed).

________. "A Demand System for Egypt—Estimation Results and Scenario Analysis for Alternative Food Price Policies." Institute of Agricultural Economics, University of Göttingen, December 1981 (mimeographed).

________. "Effects of Food Aid in Recipient Countries: Egypt and Bangladesh, a Comparative Study." *Economics (Biannual Collection of Recent German Contributions to the Field of Economic Science)* 26 (No. 2, 1982): 18-47.

Braun, Joachim von and Haen, Hartwig de. "Egypt and the Enlargement of the EEC: Impact on the Agricultural Sector." *Food Policy* 7 (February 1982): 46-56.

Bruton, Henry J. "Four Issues of Economic Policy in Egypt." Economics Study Unit, Ministry of Economy, Foreign Trade and Economic Cooperation, Cairo, 1980 (mimeographed).

Cuddihy, William. *Agricultural Price Management in Egypt.* World Bank Staff Working Paper 388. Washington, D.C.: World Bank, 1980.

Currie, J. M.; Murphy, J. A.; and Schmitz, A. "The Concept of Economic Surplus and Its Use in Economic Analysis." *The Economic Journal* 81 (December 1971): 741-799.

Davis, O. A.; Dempster, M. A. H.; and Wildavsky, A. "A Theory of the Budgetary Process." *American Political Science Review* 60 (September 1966): 529-547.

de Janvry, Alain; Siam, Gamal; and Gad, Osman. "Forced Deliveries: Their Impact on the Marketed Surplus and the Distribution of Income in Egyptian Agriculture." Economics Working Paper 38, Agricultural Development Systems Project, Ministry of Agriculture, Cairo, and the University of California-Berkeley, Cairo, September 1981.

Dethier, J. J. and Esfahani, M. "Macro-effects of Alternative Price Policies in Egypt." Economics Working Paper 188, Agricultural Development Systems Project, Ministry of Agriculture, Cairo, and the University of California-Berkeley, Cairo, September 1981.

Eckaus, Richard S.; McCarthy, F. D.; and Mohie el-Din, A. "Multi-Sector General Equilibrium Policy Models for Egypt." Development Research and Technology Planning Centre, Cairo University, 1979 (mimeographed).

Eckaus, Richard S. and Mohie el-Din, A. "Consequences of Changes in Food Subsidy Policies in Egypt." Working Paper 265. Department of Economics, Massachusetts Institute of Technology, Cambridge, Mass., April 1980.

Egypt, Economic Conference, Cairo, February 13-15, 1982. Various papers. (In Arabic.)

Egypt, Central Agency for Public Mobilization and Statistics. "Annual Trade Statistics." Cairo, various years (mimeographed). (In Arabic.)

________. "Consumer Cost of Living Indexes for Rural and Urban Areas." Cairo, various years (mimeographed). (In Arabic.)

________. *Family Budget Survey, 1958/59.* Cairo: CAPMAS, 1961.

________. *Family Budget Survey, 1964/65.* Cairo: CAPMAS, 1972.

________. *Family Budget Survey, 1974/75.* Cairo: CAPMAS, 1978.

________. "Open Market Prices for Urban and Rural Areas, 1965-1981." Cairo, n.d. (mimeographed).

________. *Population and Development.* Cairo: CAPMAS, 1978.

________. *Statistical Yearbook of Egypt.* Cairo: CAPMAS, 1980.

Egypt, Ministry of Agriculture, Institute of Agricultural Economics, Research, and Statistics. "Production Statistics." Cairo, 1982 (mimeographed).

Egypt, Ministry of Agriculture and the U.S. Agency for International Development. *Strategies for Accelerating Agricultural Development.* Cairo: Ministry of Agriculture/USAID, 1982.

Egypt, Ministry of Economy. "Egypt: Macroeconomic Performance, Problems and Prospects." Cairo, 1981 (mimeographed).

Egypt, Ministry of Economy, Foreign Trade, and Economic Cooperation. "Policy Study on Pricing and Taxation of Major Alternative Agricultural Crops." Cairo, 1980 (mimeographed).

Egypt, Ministry of Finance. "Statistics on Government Budget." Cairo, n.d. (mimeographed).

Egypt, Ministry of Planning. "Statistics of Public Agricultural Investment, 1965-1980." Cairo, 1982 (mimeographed).

Egypt, Ministry of Supply and Home Trade. "Statistics on Fixed Consumer Prices, Government Distribution of Food, Import Quantities and Cost." Cairo, n.d. (mimeographed).

__________. "Trade Statistics." Cairo, 1982 (mimeographed).

Egypt, Principal Bank for Development and Agricultural Investment, Storage and Marketing Divisions. Unpublished materials.

Egyptian Gazette, June 14, 1980, pp. 1-2.

Esfahani, Hadi and Sarris, Alexander H. "Agricultural Supply Response for the Main Crops in Egypt." Economics Working Paper 35, Agricultural Development Systems Project, Ministry of Agriculture, Cairo, and the University of California-Berkeley, Cairo, August 1981.

Fitch, James B. and Aziz, Afaf A. "Multiple Cropping Intensity in Egyptian Agriculture: A Study of its Determinants." Research Paper 5, Microeconomic Study of the Egyptian Farm System, Ministry of Agriculture, Cairo, October 1980.

Fitch, James B.; Gandi, A.; and el-Gabely, M. "The Cropping System for Maize in Egypt: Survey Findings and Implications for Policy and Research." Paper presented to FAO workshop on "Improved Farming Systems in the Nile Valley," Cairo, May 1979.

Fitch, James B. and Soliman, Ibrahim. "The Livestock Economy in Egypt: An Appraisal of the Current Situation." Cairo, 1982 (mimeographed).

Frey, Bruno S. "Politico-economic Models and Cycles." *Journal of Public Economics* 9 (April 1978): 203-220.

Ghaffar, Ahmed Abdel. First Undersecretary, Ministry of Supply and Home Trade, Egypt. Personal communications, 1981-82.

Gotsch, Carl H. and Dyer, Wayne M. "Rhetoric and Reason in the Egyptian 'New Lands' Debate." *Food Research Institute Studies* 18 (No. 2, 1982): 129-148.

Goueli, Ahmed. "Food Security Program in Egypt." In *Food Security for Developing Countries,* pp. 143-157. Edited by Alberto Valdés. Boulder, Colo.: Westview Press, 1981.

Grosse-Rueschkamp, Alois. "Optimal Planning of Feed Mix Industries in Egypt." Ph.D. thesis, University of Bonn, 1979. (In German.)

Habashi, Nabil T.; Fitch, J. B.; and Rehiwi, S. "Egypt's Agricultural Cropping Pattern: A Review of the System by which it is Managed and its Relationship to Price Policy." Research Paper 4, Microeconomic Study of the Egyptian Farm System, Ministry of Agriculture, Cairo, November 1980.

Hansen, Bent and Nashashibi, Karim. *Foreign Trade Regimes and Economic Development: Egypt.* New York: National Bureau of Economic Research, 1975.

Hansen, Bent and Radwan, Samir. *Employment Opportunities and Equity in a Changing Economy: Egypt in the 1980s.* Geneva: International Labour Office, 1982.

Hassan, Ahmed. "Cooperative Marketing and Compulsory Deliveries of Some Agricultural Crops." Institute of National Planning, Cairo, 1982 (mimeographed).

el-Hindy, Mohamed K. "Food Systems Development in Egypt." Economics Working Paper 58, Agricultural Development Systems Project, Ministry of Agriculture, Cairo, and the University of California-Berkeley, Cairo, December 1981.

Ikram, Khalid. *Egypt: Economic Management in a Period of Transition.* Baltimore, Md.: Johns Hopkins University Press, 1980.

Imam, Shawky and Fitch, James B. "Wheat Farming System in Egypt." Cairo, 1978 (mimeographed).

Ingram, J. C. and Moursi, T. "Treating Berseem as a Traded Good in the Calculation of Social Returns." Economics Working Paper 18, Agricultural Development Systems Project, Ministry of Agriculture, Cairo, and the University of California-Berkeley, Cairo, May 1981.

International Food Policy Research Institute. *Food Needs of Developing Countries: Projections of Production and Consumption to 1990.* Research Report 3. Washington, D.C.: IFPRI, 1977.

International Labour Organisation/United Nations Development Programme. "Employment Opportunities and Equity in a Changing Economy, Egypt in the 1980s." Draft report of the ILO/UNDP Employment Strategy Mission, 1980 (mimeographed).

International Wheat Council. *International Wheat Agreement: 1981,* London: International Wheat Council, n.d.

Kutcher, Gary P. "The Agro-Economic Model." Master Plan for Water Resources Development and Use, Technical Report 16, Cairo, May 1980 (mimeographed).

Lesourne, J. *Cost-Benefit Analysis and Economic Theory.* Amsterdam and Oxford: Elsevier-North Holland, 1975.

Lutz, Ernst and Scandizzo, Pasquale L. "Price Distortions in Developing Countries: A Bias against Agriculture." *European Review of Agricultural Economics* 7 (No. 1, 1980): 5-27.

Misr Dairy Company. Unpublished data. Cairo, 1979.

Mohie el-Din, Yahya. First Undersecretary, Ministry of Agriculture, Egypt. Personal communications, 1981-82.

Moustafa, Rasmia; Abdou, D.; Gardener, B. O.; and Green, R. "A Welfare Analysis of Price Policy for Wheat and Wheat Products in Egypt." Economics Working Paper 48, Agricultural Development Systems Project, Ministry of Agriculture, Cairo, and the University of California-Berkeley, Cairo, 1981.

Musgrave, Richard A. and Musgrave, Peggy B. *Public Finance in Theory and Practice.* Tokyo: McGraw-Hill Kogakusha, 1973.

Nasr, Mamdouh M. "Farmers' Supply Response within the Egyptian System of Government Acreage Planning." Ph.D. thesis, Institute of Agricultural Economics, University of Göttingen, 1983. (In German.)

Nassar, Saad; el-Amir, M. R.; and Moustafa, A. A. "Determinants of Agricultural Price Policy in Egypt." Economics Working Paper 50, Agricultural Development Systems Project, Ministry of Agriculture, Cairo, and the University of California-Berkeley, Cairo, 1982.

Newberg, R. R. "Fertilizer Subsector Assessment: Egypt." Multinational Agribusiness Systems, Washington, D.C., 1979 (mimeographed).

Pacific Consultants. "New Lands Productivity in Egypt. Its Technical and Economic Feasibility." Washington, D.C., 1980 (mimeographed).

Page, John M. *Shadow Prices for Trade Strategy and Investment Planning in Egypt.* World Bank Staff Working Paper 521. Washington, D.C.: World Bank, 1982.

Pick's Currency Yearbook, various issues. New York: Franz Pick Publishing Co., various years.

Radwan, Samir and Lee, Eddy. "The Anatomy of Rural Poverty, Egypt 1977." World Employment Programme, Geneva, 1980 (mimeographed).

Richards, Alan. *Egypt's Agricultural Development 1800-1980: Technical and Social Change.* Boulder, Colo.: Westview Press, 1982.

Sarris, Alexander H. "Food Security and Agricultural Production Strategies Under Risk in Egypt." Working Paper 249, Division of Agricultural Sciences, University of California, Berkeley, March 1983 (mimeographed).

Scobie, Grant M. *Food Subsidies in Egypt: Their Impact on Foreign Exchange and Trade.* Research Report 40. Washington, D.C.: International Food Policy Research Institute, 1983.

__________. *Government Policies and Food Imports: The Case of Wheat in Egypt.* Research Report 29. Washington, D.C.: International Food Policy Research Institute, 1981.

Soliman, Ibrahim. "Red Meat Price Policy in Egypt." Economics Working Paper 62, Agricultural Development Systems Project, Ministry of Agriculture, Cairo, and the University of California-Berkeley, Cairo, 1982.

Soliman, Ibrahim; Fitch, J. B.; and Aziz, N. A. "The Role of Livestock Production on the Egyptian Farm." Economics Working Paper 85, Agricultural Development Systems Project, Ministry of Agriculture, Cairo, and the University of California-Berkeley, Cairo, July 1982.

Taylor, Lance. "Food Subsidies in Egypt." Department of Economics, Massachusetts Institute of Technology, Cambridge, Mass., October 1979 (mimeographed).

Waterbury, John. *Hydropolitics of the Nile Valley.* Syracuse, N.Y.: Syracuse University Press, 1979.

World Bank. *Arab Republic of Egypt: Domestic Resource Mobilization and Growth Prospects for the 1980s.* Report 3123EGT. Washington, D.C.: World Bank, 1980.

__________. *Arab Republic of Egypt: Economic Management in a Period of Transition.* Vol. 6. Washington, D.C.: World Bank, 1978.

World Food Programme Office. Unpublished data. Cairo, 1982.

Wally, Youssef; el-Kholei, Osman; Abbas, Mohamad; and Heady, Earl O. *Strategy for Agricultural Development in the Eighties for the Arab Republic of Egypt.* International Development Series Report No. 9. Ames, Iowa: Iowa State University, 1982.

Zaglui, E. A. "Some Proposals to Reduce Agricultural Subsidies." Ministry of Agriculture Paper 6, Cairo, 1979 (mimeographed).

Joachim von Braun has been a researcher at IFPRI since 1981. Hartwig de Haen is a professor of agricultural economics at the University of Göttingen in the Federal Republic of Germany.